THE TWO THOUSAND ISLES

A SHORT ACCOUNT OF THE PEOPLE, HISTORY AND CUSTOMS OF THE MALDIVE ARCHIPELAGO

By

T. W. HOCKLY

WITH PLATES

GYAN

Published by

Gyan Publishing House
5, Ansari Road
Daryaganj, New Delhi-110002
Phone: 011-47034999, 9811692060
E-mail: books@gyanbooks.com

Distribution Network
gyanbooks.com
India, USA, Canada, UK, Australia, France

ISBN : 978-81-212-4177-9 (PB)
First Published, London, 1935

2nd Impression 2020

Printed at: Gyan Press, Delhi.

The Two Thousand Isles
Author: T. W. Hockly

THE TWO THOUSAND ISLES

A SHORT ACCOUNT OF THE PEOPLE, HISTORY AND CUSTOMS OF THE MALDIVE ARCHIPELAGO

By

T. W. HOCKLY

WITH PLATES

"*Voyager en toutes sortes de bateaux c'est la vie.*"

H. F. & G. WITHERBY
326, HIGH HOLBORN, LONDON, W.C.

BUGGALOW "NIRANI" OUTWARD BOUND

(*Frontispiece*)

THE TWO THOUSAND ISLES

A SHORT ACCOUNT OF THE PEOPLE, HISTORY AND CUSTOMS OF THE MALDIVE ARCHIPELAGO

T. W. HOCKLY

WITH PLATES

ASIAN EDUCATIONAL SERVICES
NEW DELHI ★ CHENNAI ★ 2003

ASIAN EDUCATIONAL SERVICES

* 31, HAUZ KHAS VILLAGE, NEW DELHI - 110016
  Tel : 2656-0187, 2656-8594 Fax : 011-2649-4946, 2685-5499
  e-mail : asian_jj@vsnl.com / aes_publications@yahoo.co.in

* 5, SRIPURAM FIRST STREET, CHENNAI - 600 014
  Tel : 2811-5040 Fax : 044-2811-1291
  e-mail : asianeds@md3.vsnl.net.in

www.asianeds.com

Price: Rs. 395
First Published : London, 1935
AES Reprint : New Delhi, 2003
ISBN : 81-206-1731-2

Published by J. Jetley
for ASIAN EDUCATIONAL SERVICES
31, Hauz Khas Village, New Delhi - 110 016.
Processed by AES Publications Pvt. Ltd., New Delhi-110016
Printed at Chaudhary Offset Process, DELHI - 110 051

FOREWORD

THIS book is not intended to be a treatise on the Maldive Islands—that *terra incognita*—but is simply the narrative of a visit to these islands by the author.

The Maldive Archipelago is a group of coral islands and atolls in the Indian Ocean near the Equator. . Isolated more or less as the inhabitants are from the rest of the world except for communication with Ceylon and India, chiefly by dhows or buggalows and their own primitive sailing craft, they have retained nearly all their original customs and traditions.

They are ruled over by a Sultan who is styled "King of Thirteen Provinces and Twelve-thousand Islands". The country has maintained its independence, and, although now under the suzerainty of the Government of Ceylon, it formulates its own laws. There has been little or no change in the general condition of the people since the Frenchman Pyrard was shipwrecked there early in the 17th Century. The people are undoubtedly of Aryan or Sinhalese origin, and are a hardy sea-faring race.

FOREWORD

Finally, I should like to take this opportunity of expressing my gratitude to the following individuals or firms who have so kindly lent me some of the photographs for reproduction in this book: H. V. Cartwright, C. C. Woolley, c.c.s., J. A. Darby, K. Adamaly, A. H. Abeyaratne, Messrs. John & Co., and "The Times of Ceylon".

T. W. H.

CONTENTS

PLATES

AUTHOR'S NOTE

Since the foregoing chapters were written several events of interest have occurred at Male.

Abdul Majid Didi returned to Male early in April, 1934, and was accorded, I understand, a welcome by the Maldivians little short of regal.

Towards the end of September Abdul Majid Didi left Male for Colombo en route to Egypt to visit his son. Hardly had he left Colombo for Egypt when, on the 2nd October, 1934, the unconstitutional conduct of the Sultan in wilfully interfering with the administration of justice, and for acting contrary to his vow to follow the Constitution, necessitated his dethronement by the people of the Maldives in accordance with Article 51 of the Maldivian Constitution.

It appears that the Minister of Home Affairs, Muhammad Farid Didi Effendi, who is also Prime Minister of the Maldive Islands, was informed that certain persons were convening secret meetings which had as their object the destruction of the New Constitution inaugurated in December, 1932.

Warrants were issued for the arrest of four persons in this respect. It was learnt from the arrested persons that there were others involved in the plot to destroy the Constitution. It was further alleged that among these others were four servants of Prince Hasan Izzudin, the son of the Sultan, who it will be remembered returned to Male in December, 1933. Apparently the Prince had interested himself on behalf of certain individuals who had been previously deported.

When officials of the Ministry of Home Affairs attempted to arrest the four servants of the Prince the latter refused to allow their arrest. He is said to have come out with his father, the Sultan, and to have informed the officials and the people gathered together that if his servants were arrested they would have also to arrest the Sultan and himself. It is stated that the Prince had then cried out asking whether they wanted the Constitution or his father and himself. The people replied that they wanted the Constitution.

Steps were then taken to effect the dethronement of the Sultan.

The "Revolution" was of an entirely bloodless character, I understand, and was not followed by any disorder.

I was told that the Sultan had left the palace and that he and his son are at present residing in a private house belonging to the former.

AUTHOR'S NOTE

The Government of Ceylon was duly and officially notified of the dethronement of the Sultan by the Maldivian Representative in Ceylon, Husain Hilmy Didi Effendi. The Maldivian Prime Minister, Muhammad Farid Didi, has himself issued a statement to the effect that " the proceedings regarding the dethronement were carried out in a most orderly manner, and peace and contentment are generally prevailing throughout the Maldives.

" The question of a successor to the throne will be discussed in due time and until a new Sultan can be appointed the Members of the Cabinet will administer the Government ".

Such is the position at present and will doubtless remain thus until the return from Egypt of Abdul Majid Didi.

There are several candidates for the throne among the close relatives of the ex-Sultan.

The question of elegibility and other matters would, of course, require to be examined carefully before arriving at any final decision.

I question, however, whether it will be worth while to select a successor to the ex-Sultan. Prince Izzudin has apparently by his action forfeited any chance he might have had of succeeding his father.

The Maldive Islands would, in my opinion, be far better off should there be any difficulty in finding a suitable successor who would reign constitutionally, if the people were to declare for a small republic under the suzerainty of the Ceylon Government.

The position of the ex-Sultan and his son Prince Izzudin, is rather anomalous at the moment.

One thing is certain I imagine, and that is they will neither of them be allowed to reside indefinitely in Male. On the other hand, if they elected to go and live in Ceylon this might also be undesirable from the point of view of the Maldivian Government as they might become the focus of intrigues having a restoration as their object.

It is more probable that both the ex-Sultan and his son will eventually be relegated to some other island in the Archipelago sufficiently remote from Male to prevent any possibility of either or both of them staging a " come-back ".

One cannot help feeling some regret for the ex-Sultan, that he should have been dethroned after an uninterrupted reign of over thirty-one years.

Apparently, however, the hasty and unconsidered action of the Prince in emulating Joshua by asking the people to " choose you this day whom ye will serve " had tended to precipitate the crisis.

Ceylon, 11th December, 1934.

CHAPTER I

THE BUGGALOW

A GENTLE breeze was blowing from the south-west. But for the slap and swish of the water on the ship's side, the creak of the sail ropes in the blocks, there was not a sound except for the helmsman behind me crooning a song very softly.

I lay on the poop deck of the buggalow, stretched out on a sleeping mat. Above me were the stars shining brilliantly from a sky of deep indigo.

At last I had realized my wish, and here I was voyaging in a buggalow to the Maldives.

The Maldive Islands, according to the last Census Report of the Ceylon Government, are a group of coral islands in the Indian Ocean situated some four hundred miles to the south-west of Ceylon, and lie between 72° 33′ and 73° 44′ east longitude and between 7° 6′ north latitude and 0° 42′ south latitude.

The most northerly island lies about three hundred and fifty miles from Cape Comorin, and Male* Island is about four hundred and fifteen miles from Colombo.

* Pronounced Malé.

THE TWO THOUSAND ISLES

The number of inhabited islands of the Maldive Archipelago according to the Census returns was two hundred and seventeen. There is no record of the number of uninhabited islands, but it is reported that they are more than two thousand in number.

The islands are grouped together in clusters called atolls; most of these, with the exception of the northern atolls, are surrounded by a barrier reef which serves as a natural protection.

In Vol. I, p. 95, of the Hakluyt Society's translation of Pyrard it is stated that "within each of these enclosures (atolls) are the islands great and small in number almost infinite. The natives informed me that there were as many as 12,000 but my notion is that there is not the appearance of so great a number, and that they say 12,000 to indicate an incredible number which cannot be counted. Yet true it is that there is an endless number of little ones which are mere sandbanks, altogether uninhabited. Moreover, the King of the Maldives puts this number among his titles for he called himself *Sultan Ibrahim dolos assa ral tera atholon*—that is to say Sultan King of thirteen provinces and 12,000 isles".

I understand, however, that *Sultan Ibrahim tera atholu dolos has ra'a* is more correct. The common term used by the people is *tera atholu bara has ra'a.*

When I first came to Ceylon some few years

before I used often to watch the buggalows either at anchor in Colombo harbour, or with their white sails spread, arriving in port or sailing away to the south-west.

The buggalow or *bagala,* as it is sometimes called, is a wooden craft, lateen rigged, with two masts raking forward. In appearance it resembles an Arab dhow with high poop and counter and considerable sheer amidships. Below the poop deck is accommodation for baggage, and stores. The crew usually keep their belongings there. Abaft this there is a cabin of sorts. The average size of a buggalow is about eighty feet in length and about twenty feet beam, the tonnage varying between one hundred and a hundred and forty tons gross.

At first I was able to obtain but little information with regard to the seemingly mysterious outgoings and in-comings of these craft.

Being fond of travel, especially by sea, I determined that some day I would make a voyage to the Maldive Islands in one of them. A friend of mine, long resident in Ceylon, whom I asked for particulars as to the probable length of the voyage to the Maldive Islands from Colombo, told me that to go there in a sailing vessel would probably mean an absence of months. That he understood the buggalows voyaged there when the wind was in favour during the north-east monsoon, but had to remain at the Maldives until the advent of the south-west monsoon. This rather cooled my enthusiasm for making such a voyage. I merely mention this *en passant* as showing the more or less hazy idea of the majority of Ceylon residents with regard to these islands as a *terra incognita.*

It was only after I had been in Ceylon for some considerable time and when I had come to know several Borah merchants in Colombo that I learned more about the probable time which would be occupied on the voyage.

The Borah merchants of Colombo are wealthy Mohammedan traders of the Shiah sect, who have originally come from Bombay and the Kathiawar coast of India, and settled in Ceylon. Besides having large landed interests in the island such as tea, rubber and coconut estates, and valuable house property in Colombo, they carry on a considerable business as importers of rice from India and Burma. They have also for many years traded with the Maldives, many of them owning their own buggalows. In these vessels they export rice, kerosene oil, sugar, cotton piece goods, and other articles for the use of the Maldivians. These goods are usually exchanged by them on a system of barter, and their argosies return laden with dried Maldive fish—a trade in which the Borahs have for a long time virtually held a monopoly in Ceylon—coconuts, copra, and, occasionally, tortoiseshell.

The Borah is a shrewd fellow and a keen

business man. He has not been slow in taking full advantage of this trade.

Dried Maldive fish is much in request by the Ceylonese, both rich and poor. It always commands a price in Colombo which more than amply repays the Borah traders. The Maldives have, indeed, proved an El Dorado for them. Their courage and acumen in establishing their trade in Male—the official capital of the Maldives, and the distributing centre of the Archipelago, have been amply rewarded. They have reaped a golden harvest for their pioneer work. One has only to look round Colombo and see the immense wealth which has accrued to them, thanks chiefly to this particular trade.

As regards the Maldivians themselves, in matters of trade and business they are mere unsophisticated children. This is, of course, due to their isolated position, lack of adequate transport, and means of communication with the outside world. They are a comparatively primitive people and lack the astuteness of the Borahs.

The Frenchman Pyrard, who was wrecked in the Maldives in the seventeenth century, states in his memoirs that it is a common saying among the Maldivians that whoever trades with them becomes rich whilst they themselves remain poor. Perhaps, though, they are happier so, for what one has never had one never misses.

As I learned from the Borah merchants that

the voyage by buggalow from Colombo to Male and back could be accomplished within a month or six weeks, I decided I would make the journey.

Shortly afterwards, finding I was able to get away for such a period, I called on one of the Borahs, a friend of mine, who was the owner of two or three buggalows. At first when I told him I wished to make the voyage in one of his vessels he could hardly believe I was in earnest, and, in fact, was rather inclined to smile at the idea.

"Sahib", said he to me, "you can never make the journey in a buggalow. The life and conditions on board would be far too rough and uncomfortable, more especially in bad weather. I myself have made the voyage once, many years ago, but Allah forbid that I should have to do so again."

When, however, he saw that I meant what I said and that I was quite prepared to rough it, he was kind enough to offer me a free passage to Male and back in one of his ships which was due to sail in a fortnight's time.

Having thanked him and accepted his offer, I began to make preparations for the voyage. I bought some stores, but I was determined only to use them when necessity arose and to fare the same as the ship's company.

As Colombo is blessed with a pure and abundant water supply the buggalows usually fill up their tanks before sailing with sufficient water to last the round voyage as the water obtainable in Male is not too good and inclined to be brackish. When I learned this I took as a precaution for use ashore at Male a sufficient supply of fresh water in new kerosene oil tins.

The next question was to obtain an official firman from the Ceylon Government, which has suzerain rights over the Maldives, to visit the islands. This necessitated a visit to the Secretariat where I received a letter of introduction in the name of the Ceylon Government addressed to the Government of the Maldives. I had then to call on the Maldivian Representative in Ceylon, Abdul Hamid Didi Effendi, who received me with every courtesy. He furnished me with a letter to his brother, Abdul Majid Didi Effendi, the Prime Minister and Chief Treasurer to His Highness the Sultan. I found Abdul Hamid Didi a most charming personality. Besides speaking perfect English he spoke fluent Hindustani. He informed me that I should find no difficulty with regard to language at Male as most of the Court Officials spoke Hindustani. Long residence in India had made me quite conversant with this language. He also assured me that I should receive every courtesy and attention during my visit.

As Mr. H. C. P. Bell of the Ceylon Civil Service (retired) had previously visited the Maldives in connection with historical and archæological research and is rightly considered to be the foremost living European authority on these islands, I arranged to call on him at his residence in Kandy with a view to obtaining any information which might be of use to me.

Bell first visited the Maldives in 1879, and thereafter his "Report on the Maldive Islands" was published as a Sessional Paper by the Ceylon Government in 1881, and contains very valuable information with regard to these islands and their inhabitants.

After his retirement he was attached as Archæologist to the Deputation despatched by the Ceylon Government to Male in January, 1920, for the purpose of investing His Highness the Sultan of the Maldives with the Most Distinguished Order of St. Michael and St. George.

On this last occasion Mr. Bell arrived in Male by H.M.S. "Comus", on January 24th, 1920, and left for Ceylon on his return voyage in the S.S. "Lady McCallum" on the 18th February of the same year.

Thereafter he wrote his "Report on a visit to Male", which was also published as a Sessional Paper by the Ceylon Government in 1921.

Subsequently, he again visited the Maldives in 1922 and stayed there from January to September of that year. During this period he conducted extensive excavations in several of the more southern atolls of the Archipelago. His discoveries have been of great importance as bearing on the question of Buddhist remains.

Several large *dagobas* or Buddhist shrines enclosing relics were unearthed and also very ancient inscriptions carved on stone in Sanskrit and Pali. These date back in many instances thousands of years and to a period contemporaneous with the buried cities of Anuradhapura and Polonaruwa in Ceylon, when they were flourishing towns of vast extent with teeming populations.

Mr. Bell was most kind when I saw him and gave me a great deal of information culled from his own wide experience which, besides being intensely interesting, proved of great value and assistance to me and I am deeply grateful to him.

All my preparations for the journey now having been completed all that was left for me was to board the vessel.

It was in the early afternoon of the 16th April, 1926, when I went on board the buggalow "Nurani" and soon settled down with my servant and belongings. The Borah owner with some of his friends came to see me off. They very kindly brought with them a generous supply of fresh fruit and vegetables for my use. Having commended me to the care of the *Naukhoda** or ship's captain and handed me a letter to his representatives in Male he bade me good-bye.

We then proceeded to up anchor, which took some little time, this being done by hand. Then we swung round and the crew began to unfurl the forward lateen sail. This was soon shaken

* lit. god of the ship.

out and the ship started on her voyage down the harbour. At first we moved almost imperceptibly but soon gained more speed. We passed the breakwater and were then on the open sea. Many fishing craft were met with speeding along with their brown sails and quaint outriggers. The Sinhalese fishermen in their wide straw hats were intent on their toil.

Although the sea was comparatively smooth, with but a light wind, the buggalow began to bow and nod to it.

Our cargo was varied and consisted chiefly of rice, onions, piece goods, kerosene oil, and bales of gunny bags for dried fish and copra.

The second lateen sail was next hoisted, and we began to make more way.

I had taken up my quarters on the poop deck. An awning of hessian cloth had been rigged across it which partially afforded some shelter from the sun. There was no room for a stretcher, but I had brought a sleeping mat and bedding with me. I was able, however, to find a place for a small deck chair.

Knowing that all the inhabitants of the Maldives were orthodox Mohammedans of the Sunni sect I had decided it would be better to take my Malay servant, Jamaldin, with me. He had never been to sea before and now began to suffer badly from sea-sickness, though he tried his best not to show it at first. It was not long before he was completely floored and I had to see to him.

Later in the afternoon, but sometime before sunset, Rahiman, one of the crew, a cheery youth, came with my food. This consisted of a plateful of boiled rice, curried fish, and some *dal,* or boiled lentils. There was also a pickle of chillies and limes. It all tasted very good. He told me this was the last meal of the day for everyone, and was usually eaten between four and five o'clock.

The food was cooked for all in a primitive stove in the caboose on the forward deck by one of the Hindu crew, the Mohammedans eating their portion separately. Rahiman, who was a Muslim, had been detailed to look after my wants. Of the ship's crew of fourteen, four were Muslims, and the others, including Jiwa, the old *Naukhoda,* were Hindus from the Kathiawar coast in the Gulf of Kutch, and subjects of " Ranji ".

The diet was practically a vegetarian one, for although the Hindus were not of a very high caste and could indulge in fish; meat, poultry and eggs were taboo for them. Before dusk fell there was a most gorgeous sunset. The sun sank in a blood-red blaze and as the after-glow came on the whole horizon became suffused with the most delicate tints. The fleecy clouds took on a pale grey, the sky forming a background of delicate rose, and further to the east a pale lemon melting into a light shade of peacock green. The stars began to come out, one by one, till they formed a canopy above us. On this the first day of the voyage we were right in the track of steamers. At night their lights could be seen twinkling hospitably in the distance.

For fear of fire the buggalow carried no lights.

Everyone not on watch turned in shortly after sunset. Around me on the deck were sheeted figures, looking like corpses prepared for burial.

As I lay on my sleeping mat, looking up at the starry sky, Rahiman came and sat near me. We spoke in Hindustani. He told me he came from Madras, but had not been there for ten or twelve years. He had been on the Maldive run ever since he was a boy. With the usual simple oriental freedom in giving such details he said he had settled in Colombo and was married and was the father of a small daughter. His young cousin, whom everyone on board called *bachha*—little one—a boy of ten, was also with him and worked more or less as a *mousse*, receiving only his food and some clothes, but no pay. I began to feel drowsy and soon dropped off to sleep.

I woke about five o'clock. The stars were beginning to dim. The crew were being woke up by the single word *uth*—Hindustani—get up. No one, however, seemed much inclined to turn over and sleep again.

The dawn broke in a wonderful flare of colour

and the sun was soon mounting the sky behind us for we were steering nearly due west. I made myself a cup of hot chocolate and smoked a cigarette. Later, I stood in the chains and had a sea-water bath by repeated dipping of a bucket overboard and sloshing its contents over me. I felt fresh and fit after this. Early morning *chapattis* or hand bread were being prepared and these served hot with the addition of a little jam or butter tasted excellent.

It was a perfect day, with a light breeze, a deep blue sea, and a turquoise sky flecked with white clouds. Nor was it a bit too hot under the awning.

At the hour of the midday meal some quite good potato and vegetable curry with rice was brought me. I enjoyed this as I was beginning to feel hungry.

The presence of a white gull betokened we were not far off land. Jiwa, the *Naukhoda,* told me Cape Comorin lay ahead of us.

From the beginning of April and sometimes even before then, the wind has begun to blow from the south-west and this meant we could only arrive at our destination by deviation and tacking.

Jiwa said we should probably take ten or twelve days to reach Malc. On our return, however, with the wind behind us, the voyage to Colombo would not be longer than four or five days. Life and conditions on a buggalow are naturally primitive. Anyone contemplating such a journey need not expect to have a steward within call to fetch a cold drink or mix a cocktail as in a liner. After all, however, it is surprising how easily one can adapt oneself to circumstances and dispense with luxuries if one is prepared to take things as they come.

Of the ship's crew, Hasan and Husain were Muslim and brothers, hailing from Minicoy in the Lacadives. They had both been serving in the ill-fated "Lady McCallum" when she foundered off the east coast of Ceylon on New Year's Day, 1926. Rahiman was the general handy man. Bachha, his cousin, was a most amusing and intelligent young *gamin*. He knew a little English and could speak Hindustani, Tamil and Sinhalese. He was both the butt and the pet of the crew, but was made to work hard and fetch and carry for everyone. He used often to go aloft like a monkey, and was quite fearless and very good natured. The *Naukhoda*, Jiwa, was a fine old Hindu between fifty and sixty and a real old salt. He told me he had been at sea for over forty years. Many a long talk I had with him and he gave me a lot of interesting information about the Maldives and the inhabitants.

He always took his turn at the wheel with the others.

His son Megji was with him, quite a promising

lad who helped him to take bearings every day—for these *Naukhodas* all understand the use of chronometer, sextant and quadrant.

Then there was Birji, another hard-bitten, grizzled old veteran, but with a great fund of quiet wit and humour. He was fond of poetry and when at the wheel, especially at night, used to croon Hindustani *gazals* and love songs of which he seemed to have quite a large repertoire. He informed me that he had been many years at sea. He had at first run away from home as a boy and joined a travelling theatrical company where he had learned most of his songs.

There was Keshwa, or *billi,* the cat, as he was called, another Hindu. A hefty young fellow about twenty-five. He was a *sukhani,* or helmsman, but very keen on fishing when off duty. The rest were all simple, kindly folk, like most sailor-men.

The rest of the voyage is taken from extracts from my diary.

17th April. Turned in early, those not on watch doing the same, and we were all soon asleep. Woke up about midnight. Another glorious night of stars. Orion on our port, and the Great Bear on the starboard quarter with the North Star glimmering low down on the horizon. Went to sleep again.

18th April. Woke at dawn. Sighted Cape Comorin about 7 a.m. and the range of hills rising up from it very barren looking and not unlike the approach to Aden from the distance, though I believe the coast is palm-fringed. Soon after we trimmed sail, rather an arduous task. All hands were hard at it, and soon we had swung round and were heading southwards shortly after 7 a.m. Enjoyed lounging on deck in nothing but a tennis shirt and pair of shorts. As I had taken care to bring a number of books with me I had plenty to occupy my mind.

19th April. The day broke fine, with the wind steady from the south-west. We were now steering in a S.S.W. direction.

Encountered a fairly heavy ground swell and the ship laboured a bit. Shortly after noon a fine *sier* fish was caught on a line which had been kept trailing behind the vessel. Old Jiwa was very pleased and said I had brought them good luck.

20th/21st April. Encountered heavy squalls about midnight on both nights accompanied by rain. We were compelled to shorten sail as the wind freshened and a heavy sea was running. Later the weather improved, the wind having abated considerably. Jamaldin, my servant, after having recovered from his first bout of sea-sickness had a bad relapse with the rough weather.

22nd April. The morning was cloudy, but cool, with a moderate wind from the S.W. A little before noon a large fish was caught, dark blue on top, with yellow sides. It must have been over twenty pounds in weight. It proved excellent eating, the flesh being white and flaky. At night a large fish, or, perhaps, a shark, carried away part of the line which was of stout log line, the trace being of thin brass wire.

23rd April. Another large fish was hooked in the morning but in attempting to gaff it with a boat-hook, the line broke and it got away. About nine o'clock in the morning we passed quite near to and spoke with a buggalow homeward bound to Ceylon. The *Naukhoda* after hailing the vessel shouted out a message to be given to my friends in Ceylon that I was safe and well.

24th April. Sail was trimmed about four a.m. There was a clear sky and a calm sea. Land Ho ! was shouted by the look-out man from the mast-head and about six o'clock we sighted a small island well to the south at the edge of an atoll.

The weather continued fine; and as the atoll was approached breakers could be seen extending on both sides for miles. In some places the barrier of reefs could be distinctly observed. The sea breaking over this long line of reefs was a magnificent sight; the foam-crested waves resembling a line of silver-thread from the distance, and the roar of the surf could be heard like one long continued diapason.

The island itself within the atoll which we passed

to port was only a quarter of a mile in length, with clumps of coconut trees spreading upwards and outwards. The rest of the verdure seemed composed of scrub and stunted jungle trees. The sand on the shore was peculiarly white, which is the case on all the islands as it is composed largely of powdered coral. We had to make a long detour to keep in deep water and avoid the reef.

Navigation among these atolls is ticklish work calling for clear-headedness and coolness, especially on dark, moonless nights, for there are no lights whatever to guide the mariner. A false calculation would put a ship on the reefs and she would be soon dashed to pieces in the terrific surge of the sea. I was told there is great depth of water near some of these reefs. Subsequently I have read in an official report that in some places close to the islands and reefs there is no bottom at a depth of two hundred fathoms.

As the afternoon wore on the wind gradually fell, and by the time the moon rose we were almost in a dead calm. The sails flapped idly and old Jiwa was in despair as the ship was making no headway.

It was a cloudless night. I turned in early and was asleep shortly after eight. I woke later to find Birji at the wheel. He was relating to some of the others a story about a fairy falling in love with a young and handsome prince and the consequent complications. The story seemed interminable and I dozed off again. I was awakened suddenly by the roar of breakers.

I got up and looked round. On our port bow at no great distance was a white wall of surf breaking over a reef many miles in length. The wind had improved somewhat and we were steering in a N.N.W. direction. The Great Bear was visible on our starboard side and Orion in full splendour to port. Due south could be seen the gleam of the Southern Cross. The moon had set, but the stars were bright. In the east shone the morning star making a path of light on the water. I looked at my watch; it was close on four o'clock. The steady boom of the breakers was more persistent than ever. The *Naukhoda* was on deck. He came and stood near me. " Look, Sahib," he said, " the gateway to Male."

A long barrier reef stretched away at right angles to us, behind which could be seen in the dim light small islands with clumps of trees forming dark masses like shadows in the distance. We ported helm and came parallel with the reef. As we approached nearer the roar of the surf increased.

" Where are we going to now ? " I asked.

" We shall skirt the edge of the reef, and further on there is an opening through which we shall pass," Jiwa replied.

We seemed to be coming nearer and nearer to the surf. I confess I did not feel quite comfortable as I reflected on what might happen if we were caught in the swirl and carried on to the rocks. An error of judgment or miscalculation would easily have piled us up. The old *Naukhoda* told me it was always a very anxious time, more especially on a dark night or in dirty weather when visibility was bad.

A beacon light of some sort placed at the eastern end of this reef or on the island behind it which is the southern coast of Male itself would, I think, be of great assistance to navigation.

On coming to the end of the barrier, the helm was put a-starboard and there before us lay open water. Male on our port, and the neighbouring island of Hulule on our starboard-beam looked like dark shadows with breakers at no great distance on either side of us.

We sailed in quietly, however, and ere long had described the riding lights of several other buggalows at anchor in the roadstead.

A dim glimmer of light came from Male itself.

Soon we were ranged near the other buggalows of which there were six in port. Where we lay there was hardly any tide, and the water was calm.

It was the 25th April, the tenth day after my departure from Ceylon.

Here was Male at last.

Dawn was breaking. Soon it was sunrise, and the light of a new day revealed the surroundings.

CHAPTER II

MALE

To the south of where we were lay the town of Male. Our anchorage was about two miles distant from the shore.

To the north-east of Male are the islands of Dunidu, Funadu, and Hulule, and to the south-west another island called Viligili. West of us was another, and quite near was a smaller uninhabited island with coconut palms and undergrowth. On its southern side lay the skeleton of a buggalow—one of five—wrecked here a few years previously during a great storm.

All round us were green islands looking like uncut emeralds in a sea of sapphire.

To make fast after the sails had been furled, the starboard anchor had to be conveyed in the ship's boat to the shore on the small island near us. We had already dropped our port anchor.

The water here is deep—about eighteen to twenty fathoms by the chart.

There was but little breeze and the day promised to be hot. Hardly had we moored when the crows began to visit us, perching on the rigging and elsewhere in their usual impudent manner. The familiar call of the *koil*—the Ceylon and Indian hot-weather bird—came to us from the small island.

We were later boarded by the Port Health Officer who came alongside in a sailing boat. He seemed rather surprised to see an European on board. When I addressed him in English he excused himself but seemed more at ease when he found I could speak Hindustani. I showed him my firman from the Ceylon Government and also the letter I had received from the Maldivian Representative, and requested him to have these letters delivered for me.

They have a strict rule about quarantine in Male. Every buggalow entering the port must have completed twelve days from her last port before commencing to discharge cargo ere any-one is allowed on shore.

In spite of varying and contrary winds we had made a quick passage for the time of year from Colombo, but no advantage was gained by this as it meant a delay of two more days before the ship's cargo could be handled.

It was difficult to judge what Male was like at a distance of two miles, but as far as I could see through my binoculars it seemed quite populous. Most of the houses and warehouses appeared to have galvanized corrugated iron roofs, though here and there some were tiled.

Male is low-lying like all the other islands, and is about a mile in length and half that distance in breadth.

To the north of where we were anchored was rather a wonderful sight. The sea continues a sapphire blue for some distance; then it shallows up as it approaches a tremendous line of reef. The colour shades off to a jade green and then to the palest acquamarine. It melts into a long silver-white streak of breakers which crash over the invisible reef with a dull roar.

The brilliant tropical sunshine of course enhances this gorgeous blend of colour, giving it a marvellous beauty.

Southwards is another stretch of sapphire water, and right in the centre of it a long streak of jade green and beyond this more sapphire blue water.

In the evening I received a State visit from Ahmad Didi Effendi Dhori Mena Kilegeafanu, to give him his full Maldivian title, extra Private Secretary to His Highness the Sultan, also Collector of Customs and Post Master General. He brought me an invitation to come on shore the following day as accommodation had been arranged for me.

There was a heavy shower of rain in the afternoon followed by a fine evening.

I turned in early but awoke about midnight in a heavy rain-storm. However, Billi got busy and soon made everything snug, giving me fresh cause to admire the innate resourcefulness and kindliness of all sailor-men, whether white or brown.

Early next morning I packed my baggage and stores.

The wonderfully clear water invited me to take a dive off the buggalow but the fear of a prowling shark at first restrained me. However, when I saw several of the crew jump in and swim around I could no longer resist the temptation to take a header. I joined them and thoroughly enjoyed my swim.

At eight o'clock Ahmad Didi came alongside in the Royal gig manned by twelve oarsmen, and requested me to accompany him ashore. My baggage was sent off in another boat.

Ahmad Didi informed me he was fifty-nine years of age. He had visited Egypt, Turkey and Greece, prior to the war. He had also spent many years at Galle in Ceylon. He spoke English quite well and also Sinhalese, but confessed he was more at home with Hindustani, so at his request we always conversed in that language.

We landed at a short wooden jetty, standing in a small harbour. Near by were the walls and battlements of an old fort. I enquired about this from Ahmad Didi and he said, "Yes, it is a fort, but what real need have we of forts here now ? Our fort is the British Navy"

I told him that H.M. King George V. had described the British Navy as " our sure shield ".

Proceeding along the jetty we came to the entrance of the town. Apparently the sight of a single white stranger caused no little stir and we were followed by a large crowd of men and boys.

Since Pyrard's time, when he spent five years in the Maldives A.D. 1602-1607, but few Europeans have visited these islands, and most of these have been shipwrecked mariners.

" Even now, except for the occasional visit to Male of a British war ship, the islands as a group are virtually unknown, though for a century or more they have been a Dependency of England's chief Crown Colony—Ceylon.

" The relations hitherto undefined between the British Government and the Sultans of the Maldive Islands were for the first time laid down clearly in a State Agreement in 1887. By this compact the Sultan—

(a) Recognized for himself and his successors the Suzerainty of the Sovereign of Great Britain over the Maldive Islands.

(b) Disclaimed all right or intention to enter into negotiations or treaty with any Foreign State except through the Ruler of Ceylon.

For its part the British Government engaged—

(c) To protect the Maldive Islands from all foreign enemies.

(d) To abstain as far as possible from intervention in the local affairs and disputes of the Group.

This Agreement was confirmed by a letter dated 16th December, 1887, from the Sultan Muhammad Mu'in-ud-din II. to the Ceylon Government."

I am quoting from Bell.

We passed through a gateway leading to the residential quarter and walked straight on for a couple of hundred yards. The roads are all of white coral sand and I have never seen any place kept cleaner. There were several small shops and a few houses where plantain, papaya and mango trees, and many shrubs were flourishing most luxuriously. Although the soil is only coral sand and no manuring is carried out it seems to possess marvellously fecund properties.

The poorer inhabitants have their houses walled from the street with mats or *cadjans* made from palm leaves, about six to seven feet in height. Every little dwelling stands in its own compound. They are roofed either with *cadjans* or corrugated iron sheets.

We stopped at a gate set in a porch, not unlike a lichgate, which Ahmad Didi opened and we entered. Within was a small garden of crotons and other shrubs. Beyond was a neat little bungalow comparatively newly-built with a verandah in front. Ahmad Didi informed me that although it was assigned as a residence for his brother Abdul Majid Didi it was lent by him on occasions for guests of the State. He mentioned that Mr. H. C. P. Bell had stayed here on the occasion of his visit in 1920.

Everything was spotlessly clean and the furniture good and adequate. Ahmad Didi asked me to consider this my home during my visit to Male.

There was a centre room and two bed-rooms on the left of it, and one on the right. A small verandah looked out on the back where were out-offices, a kitchen and servants' quarters. There was another building adjoining the back verandah in which was a dining room. Outside of this a corridor led to a door through which one entered the bath room. This was a huge room more like a hall. In the centre of it was a well and bucket and a stone slab. Around it was fine white coral sand. A large divan covered with a fine Maldivian mat was in a corner on which one could disrobe or dress and behind it was a large mirror. The sand I found was as absorbent as blotting paper. Any water spilt on it dried up immediately. Sanitary arrangements are primitive, but hygienic, and very stringently enforced by the Maldivian Government, and one is reminded of the laws relating to personal hygiene as laid down by Moses for the Children of Israel—*vide* Deuteronomy XXIII and 13.

Whilst Ahmad Didi was showing me round, two Indian Borah merchants called to see me.

They were the representatives of my Borah merchant friend in Colombo, and had received a letter from him asking them to do everything to make my stay as pleasant and comfortable as possible. After a pressing invitation from them to be sure and visit them they took leave of me.

Ahmad Didi and I then returned to the Custom House near the jetty where all my luggage had been conveyed. I had only to give my assurance that what I had brought with me was for my own personal use and not for trade, after which orders were given for the luggage to be taken to the bungalow.

Having expressed a wish to have a look at the business quarter of the town Ahmad Didi told off one of his men to show me the way.

I walked along the harbour front where innumerable craft were lying. The principal business here is of course in dried fish, coir, and copra, boats bringing these to Male, as the trading centre, from the islands far and near.

Some of the boats are very bluff in the bows, whilst others are built on finer lines and have a curved horn-like prow of a distinctly Phœnician type. They carry a square rigged sail of canvas or, in many cases, of coconut matting. Several have a thatched roof astern. These craft are known as *odis*.

Smaller boats carrying a lateen sail function to

a large extent as lighters and are called *dhonis* or *machuas.*

The harbour wears an animated appearance and small boats like shallops ply hither and thither. They carry about two or at most three people and look rather like half a walnut shell, only shallower in proportion, and are called *bokuras.*

Only wooden pegs are employed in the construction of Maldivian craft. This is probably to save the expense of importing iron ones and also that the wooden nails last longer and do not eat into the timber in the same way as iron nails do through rust.

The reason given me, however, was that with wooden nails there would be no danger of any of the boats in their wanderings on the high seas being attracted to the magic magnetic island referred to in the Arabian Nights which drew the iron nails out of ships, causing these to come apart and founder in mid-ocean.

There are quite a large number of shops and warehouses near the waterside. All of them are roofed with corrugated iron. Many of them have a courtyard all roofed in where business is transacted between the Borah merchants and the islanders.

Usually a huge divan stands in one corner on which cushions or pillows are piled and here one is invited to sit. Most of these shops are owned by Indian merchants.

Many articles used by the islanders have to be imported. Cotton goods from Manchester, Holland, India and Japan, as well as cotton yarn and skeins of raw silk. Many of the women are expert weavers and some of the products from their hand looms which are kept for festas are bordered with silk and coloured with indigenous vegetable dyes. The cotton goods imported consist chiefly of *sarong* cloths of varied colours and checks, but dark blue seems to be the colour most favoured.

As no rice is grown, large quantities of this cereal are imported from India and Burma via Ceylon. Dry grains such as millet and maize are, however, successfully cultivated in several of the atolls and also many kinds of tropical vegetables.

Salt is also imported, though why this should not be manufactured locally with salt pans I cannot understand.

The only artificial light is that obtained from kerosene or "gas light" as the Maldivians call it, and coconut oil, and a large quantity of the former is imported annually.

The boats that bring in dried fish, coir and copra from the islands return home after obtaining all their requirements in Male from the Borah merchants.

The Maldivian fish, a species of tunny or bonito, when dried, smoked and cut up, look like pieces of black or brown wood and are quite as hard. This is exported in gunny bags as also is copra, the sacking being all imported from Calcutta either direct or usually through Colombo.

I was ushered upstairs by my merchant friends to the private office and dwelling rooms above their shop. The windows command a fine view of the waterside and harbour. Here I found an ample repast had already been prepared for me. The dishes were all oriental but none the less very excellent.

An extraordinarily good prawn curry cooked in coconut milk was the principal dish though there were many other curries as well. There was a kind of cake made of millet flour which was sweet and crisp and tasted very like shortbread.

Oriental hospitality is proverbial and almost overwhelming at times. Often it is most difficult to convince the host that one has eaten more than sufficient.

Afterwards I was shown over the warehouses which were quite large and extensive and at the back of the shop. I was told it was most difficult to obtain a lease of ground now-a-days in Male as the island being so small and the population being over seven thousand the congestion can be imagined.

After taking leave of the merchants I returned to the bungalow where I found my Malay boy,

Jamaldin, installed. He had opened out my luggage and laid out such things as were requisite for my use.

In the evening Ahmad Didi came to see me and enquired as to my well-being and comfort. He also conveyed the excuses of his younger brother, the Wazir or Prime Minister, Abdul Majid Didi Bodu Baderi Manikufanu, who was suffering from an attack of fever and was therefore unable to accompany him.

I had been careful previously to hand my visiting cards to Ahmad Didi to be given to His Highness, the Sultan, and to his brother the Wazir.

Ahmad Didi and I had a long talk and he told me how during the war the "Emden" had visited some of the islands and how another German ship, a raider, the "Wolf", had stored and watered at some of the out-lying islands. The Germans had paid in English gold for all they took. The islanders, seeing white men, presumed they were British. How, too, the British and Japanese war ships had called in search of the Germans.

I did not refer to the subject of the ex-Sultan, the cousin of the present ruler, who is now living in Egypt, as this was rather a delicate subject.

It appears, however, that the ex-Sultan happened to go on a Haj or pilgrimage to the Holy Places—Mecca and Medina, and was returning home via Egypt. There he married an Egyptian lady of exalted birth. Whether he dallied too long at Capua and neglected his country I know not, but at any rate his cousin has now ruled in his stead since 1903. The eldest son of the ex-Sultan is, I believe, living in Colombo in rather obscure and reduced circumstances.

The Maldivian language bears a close resemblance to Sinhalese. Bell is of opinion that in view of traces of Buddhism being found in the islands and the close affinity of language that " at a period of time still unknown to us the Maldives were colonized from Ceylon, or, as also may be possible, were colonized at the same time as Ceylon by Aryan immigrants from the Continent of India. There seems little doubt that although all the inhabitants are Mohammedans, Buddhism was at one time the chief religion of the people "

With the spread of Islam came the Arab pirates and traders and gradually everyone in the islands was converted from Buddhism to Islam. The conversion of the people to Mohammedanism dates from 1153 A.D.

There has undoubtedly been a strong infusion of Arab blood and of Dravidian as well.

With the Arabs came their negro slaves and here again an admixture of African blood has occurred. Some of the people are very dark with distinctly negroid faces and crisp woolly hair. Others have sharp-cut Arab features with light or copper-coloured skin. Others still possess a purer Aryan cast of face and resemble more the Sinhalese.

With regard to the negroid portion of the inhabitants I was informed that there is one of the islands almost solely inhabited by people of this type.

Of the women of the place I saw but few during my sojourn in Male. Although it is a Moslem country women do not go veiled, but, nevertheless, they seemed very shy and timid as deer, and run inside their houses on the approach of a stranger. The women as a rule are fairer than the men though this may be accounted for, perhaps, because they probably do not expose themselves so much to the sun, their domestic duties keeping them for longer periods indoors. They are possessed of good figures and regular features and some of the young women are distinctly attractive and good-looking.

In spite of this apparent shyness, however, I was told that chastity is not always a very strong point among them. Many are mutable in their affections and being passionate in their nature are much inclined to sexuality. There is a considerable amount of venereal disease prevalent I believe. This has, however, possibly been imported and is probably due to the men returning after a protracted stay in other ports where they have contracted such diseases and brought them back with them.

Pyrard in his " Voyage aux Indes " refers repeatedly to the laxity of morals among Maldivian women and also to the prevalence of venereal diseases even in his time.

The women wear invariably a waist-cloth, chocolate in colour, relieved by black and white stripes, called a *faili*. A smock or chemise-like upper garment reaching to the knees, chiefly of dark blue or terra cotta, with sleeves tight-fitting at the wrist and with a yoke at the neck cut fairly low, and edged with red or blue or yellow embroidery. A coloured handkerchief rolled round the coil of their thick dark hair made up into a knot on the right side of the head completes the attire.

Many bangles are worn on the wrist and the better classes also wear necklaces, ear-rings and other kinds of jewellery. Girls are dressed the same as boys until they reach nine or ten years of age, only wearing a waist-cloth and leaving the upper portion of the body bare.

In a note by Burton in his translation of the " Arabian Nights " he states that there is a saying current among the Arabs that a girl to be beautiful must be like a boy, and a boy to be beautiful must be like a girl. I daresay if this is carefully analysed there will be found a considerable amount of truth in it. It is not meant of course that a boy should look and be effeminate but would refer apparently to the features being refined. As regards the girls, even the modern occidental dress and figure accentuate the slim boyish silhouette.

Boys are usually circumcised at the age of seven.

There was a charming little girl of five or six who used frequently to come to the Borah merchants' shops. She usually wore only a waist-cloth but sometimes a short shirt as well. Everyone called her "Tuttu". She was not a bit shy and was a general favourite with everybody.

The men wear sarongs of various patterns, some of checks or of dark-coloured cotton, preferably blue or deep red. Under the sarong is worn a pair of short cotton drawers which may be of white, green, blue or other shade.

Either nothing is worn on the head or a dark chocolate-coloured cotton handkerchief tied flat with the ends protruding like bows on either side. In some few cases white turbans are worn. A short coat, half blouse, half shirt, or often just a cotton singlet completes the dress. Some of these coats have the collar starched whilst others have no collar. In length the coat reaches to a little below the waist.

No ordinary Maldivian wears or is supposed to

wear either sandals or shoes nor can an umbrella be carried. These are the prerogatives of royalty as are also, I was told, black silk or alpaca cloth.

As a race the Maldivians are not tall, and in this also they resemble the Sinhalese, though, of course, there are exceptions as there are in Ceylon. They are, however, of sturdy physique. Although inclined to be somewhat shy and reserved at first, I found them polite and friendly and kindly in their manners.

Everyone retires for the night at an early hour and night wanderers are not encouraged by the local police force. About sixty years ago I believe a rule was passed by the Maldivian Government prohibiting any foreign residents from going abroad after seven o'clock in the evening without a permit. At that time as there was no police force in existence there was a considerable amount of laxity with regard to the observance of this order. With the establishment of a police force, however, this rule has been more strictly enforced. The foreign merchants and shop-keepers are, nevertheless, allowed to repair to their mosque and outhouses at any hour during the night.

It was warm at first when I went to bed on my first night in Male, but later a cool breeze from the south sprung up. It was nice to sleep on a bed again after the hard deck of the buggalow.

There was not a mosquito to be seen. At

certain seasons, however, I was informed they are very bad.

In some of the islands where tanks for fresh water were dug the mosquitoes increased so alarmingly that these tanks had to be filled up again. In other islands mosquitoes are bad throughout the day but disappear at nightfall, whilst in others again mosquitoes are not to be seen through the day but are so bad at night that it is hardly possible for even the Maldivians themselves to sleep without a mosquito net.

I had been warned, however, of the Maldivian malaria, which attacks most new-comers to these islands. Pyrard, writing in the seventeenth century, refers to the Maldivian fever, stating that few who visit these islands escape it. He also records that "their musketos bite more severely than in any other part of the Indies".

I sincerely hoped that I should prove one of the exceptions, a hope which, unfortunately, was not realized, as I went down with a bad bout of fever shortly after my return to Ceylon.

I woke early the following morning. The weather was clear and bright with a blue sky overhead.

Fresh goat's milk had been sent to me and was a welcome addition to my morning cup of tea. Cattle are scarce in these islands as there is insufficient fodder for them. The number of goats, however, is innumerable, everyone seemingly possesses a small flock of them. They do not always thrive so well however on some of the islands in the Archipelago as they do in Male. Goats provide both milk and meat for the inhabitants. Possibly goat's milk may be one of the causes of fever as was proved to be the case some years ago in Malta. It is, however, far more likely due to the mosquito, as the fever is of a malarial type generally known as benignant tertian.

A plentiful supply of poultry and eggs is available, as also fish, fresh from the sea. All these can be obtained very cheaply.

The inhabitants, all being orthodox Muslims, such an animal as a dog is not to be seen, much less of course a pig. The fact that there are no dogs eliminates the risk of hydrophobia. They are regarded as unclean animals, and Pyrard relates that when the King of Portugal sent two dogs as a present to the king he ordered them to be drowned immediately.

The few snakes that are found are harmless. There are scorpions but not very many, and usually of small size. Centipedes, too, are found occasionally. In many of the islands however, land crabs, some of enormous size, are met with.

In the back garden of the guest house, which is practically all white sand on the surface, was a pomegranate tree bearing some fruit but not of any size. There were other shrubs and trees about, which seemed to flourish. I imagine the sub-soil is considerably better than the surface.

Fresh water is always to be found at a very shallow depth, as a rule only a matter of a few feet from the surface in most places, and, sometimes, too, within only a few feet from the sea shore. I do not think the fresh water issues from any subterranean springs. It is really nothing but sea-water for which the islands, being composed of coral and coral sand, acts as an enormous filter. The same thing obtains in most of the other islands. In some cases the water drawn up at first is found to be fresh and later becomes brackish. When this happens earth or sand is thrown into the excavation in some quantity and when more fresh water is required the filling is dug out again and for a time fresh water results. This procedure is repeated from time to time. Many wells, however, yield a permanent supply of fresh water.

As regards the coconut harvest, though a comparatively large quantity of coir yarn, copra and coconuts is exported, the nuts are usually much smaller than in Ceylon or on the Malabar coast, but the trees bear very prolifically. The salt of the sea, though beneficial, is the only fertilizer.

After a refreshing bath at the well in the bath-house I dressed and, as it was still cool, I decided to go for a stroll and have a closer look at the town.

CHAPTER III

MALE AND THE PORTUGUESE

In the centre of Male stands the Jama Masjid, or Hukuru Miskit, the principal mosque, a large building surrounded by shrines or *ziarats* of saints and also ordinary graves.

A grave with a pointed head-stone denotes the last resting place of a man, whilst rounded head-stones denote the graves of women.

The mosque itself has no particular architectural features but the minaret or *munnaru* nearby, which appears on the Maldivian stamps, is rather exceptional, and of a kind I had never seen before. It is a large, round, white tower, about, fifty feet in height. On top of this a tower of smaller diameter is superimposed on the lower one like the tier of a wedding cake. The effect is rather bizarre and in the distance might be taken for a large water tower. High up on the tower in blue lettering are written verses from the Koran and the *azan* or call to prayer in Arabic.

The Munnaru itself is comparatively modern, dating from A.D. 1674 and was built by Sultan Iskandar Ibrahim I. whose name is loved and revered to this day. He reigned for a period of nearly forty years.

There are a vast number of shrines everywhere. These are the tombs of local saints. At almost every corner one sees them with their white flags flying over them. There are also many mosques, about fifty altogether, I believe, which seems out of all proportion to the requirements of the population. Most of them have, however, been erected in honour of or endowed by some holy man.

The cemeteries are very numerous, and I should imagine it must be difficult burying the dead here when water everywhere is found so close to the surface, nor can it be very healthy having graves in such close proximity to dwellings and the water supply.

Male is so small and so much space is taken up by mosques, graveyards, and the shrines of saints, that it gave one the impression that more attention was paid to the requirements of the dead than of the living.

The best solution of the difficulty would be either cremation, the introduction of which would, of course, be impossible, being totally opposed to Moslem tenets, or to utilize a neighbouring uninhabited island for burial purposes. The latter might, however, not be feasible in stormy weather, and, furthermore, it is stated by Pyrard that " they never transport corps from one island to another, and even the king himself is buried where he happens to die ".

MINARET OF THE HUKURU MISKET; THE CHIEF MOSQUE IN MALE.

Near the great mosque are the residential quarters of the officials. The houses do not appear large and have only a ground floor, but all of them seem to be neatly and cleanly kept. Most of them have tiled roofs. Every house has a gate in the entry porch leading to a garden within, rather in the Arab style. One house, the residence of the young prince Hasan Izzuddin, has been built after the same model as many of the single storey bungalows in Colombo, even to the ornamentation of the gables. Workmen and masons were specially brought from Ceylon, I was told, to assist in building it. Incidentally, the prince received almost the whole of his education in Ceylon at the Royal College. It was doubtless built in this style because of his desires for a residence similar to many he had seen whilst living in Colombo.

After passing the house of the prince one goes through a gateway and enters a square. On the left hand and facing the harbour is an upper-storied building with a flagstaff in front of it and a verandah all round. It is a look-out house for some of the palace guards. Near it is a long two-storied building. This is the *Naubat Khana* or place where the Sultan's drums are kept, and also other musical instruments for His Highness' band.

This is a general custom in many parts of India, and the East, as I have seen the same thing at the palace entrance of many potentates and it is always known by the same name.

On certain nights in the week *beru,* or large drums, are beaten in the Naubat Khana. In the distance one hears them throb and reverberate for hours, sometimes till dawn, now in a monotonous cadence, then changing suddenly to a quick crescendo, and gradually sinking to a diminuendo, followed by a few minutes of silence, during which I imagine the performers are resting. Once more the drums throb out in the stillness of the night. Although the Sultan lives in close proximity to the Naubat Khana I suppose he has long since accustomed himself to the sound, and probably rather likes it.

Behind the Naubat Khana stands the Sultan's palace. Much of it cannot be seen from the road, but one building has plain white-washed walls and tiled roof, and another beside it appeared to be made of wood and roofed with copper sheets.

As previously stated the majority of the houses with the exception of those belonging to the officials are roofed with corrugated iron sheeting. This may, perhaps, be more permanent than if thatched with *cadjan* but the heat during the day must be intense.

The large open space or *maidan* in front of the *Naubat Khana* seems to be a favourite grazing ground for the few cattle that are about.

On the harbour side is a high wall on which

are mounted some few pieces of ordnance, but as these were all encased carefully in galvanized iron sheets I was unable to judge their size or calibre. They are only used, I believe, to fire salutes on occasion.

During my stay in Male, Ahmad Didi had many conversations with me, calling daily at the guest house and enquiring after my health and comfort. Sometimes he invited me to tea with him at his house which was near by. I have to thank him for many interesting details regarding the conditions and customs of his country.

The Maldivians themselves are a most peaceable and law-abiding race and there is little theft, and violent crime is practically unknown. Ahmad Didi accounted for this to the fact that no spirituous liquor or deleterious drugs are allowed to be imported. Even the juice of the coconut palm is only drunk absolutely fresh and must be thrown away the moment it ferments.

I suggested that there were sometimes other factors, such as jealousy, crimes arising out of the eternal triangle, but, apparently, the inhabitants take such matters philosophically. There is no jail and any thefts or disputes about land are settled by the Qazi. The offenders are either fined or sent to a distant island for stated periods of time and may not return to their homes until such period is completed.

I was told that no difference whatever was

made between the Maldivian subjects and the foreign merchants and their employees in any court of law.

In cases of proved adultery the Qazi orders the complainant to deliver a certain number of strokes as is deemed sufficient at the time for the offence on the thighs of the delinquent with a leather thong kept for the purpose of corporal punishment. Should the complainant be a weakling or old man, and lack sufficient strength to perform this duty well and efficiently, the Qazi then details a Government employee to carry out the sentence adequately. In cases of persistent and aggravated adultery both the offending parties, man and woman, are beaten. It then lies with the husband to continue to live amicably with his wife or if he so desires he can give her *talaq*, or divorce, in the easy Mohammedan way.

With regard to the leather thong itself, this is called a *durra*. It hangs on the wall of the Banderige or Treasury, in which building is also housed the Postal Department and Government Stores. In length the instrument is about two and a half feet. It consists of two or three layers of stout leather bound together, round at the end, with flat copper studs running down the sides. The haft is of lacquered wood, about ten inches long, and is continued down till it meets and grips the leather with copper studs. The thong itself is therefore twenty inches in length and has a breadth of four and a half inches. The thickness is about quarter of an inch.

It can easily be understood that when the *durra* is skilfully wielded it is capable of making most people sit up. Not having the cutting or lacerating power of a rattan cane, however, it can be applied with less harmful effect.

Rape appears to be a very rare occurrence, and for this offence the culprit, if the assault has been satisfactorily proved, has to submit himself to the *durra* as a corrective, receiving sometimes as many as fifty or even a hundred lashes.

In the rare cases of murder or homicide, the criminal's bare body is painted black and white, then palm branches are tied upright round him. Four ropes are attached to his body and at the end of each stands a man. After this he is hauled along through the streets and at the principal road junctions he is halted and details of his crime are recounted for the benefit of the populace. At each halt he receives a certain number of lashes with the *durra.* He is then deported to a distant island and must stay there as best he can with others of his kind for the remainder of his days.

Apparently no attempts at escape are made, as they are so carefully watched and the espionage system so good that the officials would at once be aware of any such attempt.

The punishment above described bears some

resemblance to the procedure adopted by the ancient Sinhalese Kings of Ceylon for minor offences and described in the Lak Raja Lo Sirita which has been translated by Dr. G. P. Malalasekera. It reads as follows:—

". . . . . a man may be fined or imprisoned or put in chains or he may be handed over to the town police to be decorated with *ratmal* or red flowers (probably hibiscus), bones of dead oxen, and with his hands tied behind him to be flogged till his skin sticks to the bamboo cane, while all the time he is made to proclaim aloud his crime as he is driven through the four streets to the accompaniment of the beating of drums. Or he may be banished to the fever-stricken districts of Bintenne, Badulla, or Telipeha."

One wonders what punishment was meted out to those wretches found guilty of serious crimes.

I enquired how the roads and streets were kept so clean, a fact I had noticed on the first day I arrived, and was told the rule is that the residents on one side of a road must keep their half of it swept, a similar duty devolving on the dwellers opposite.

The fruit which is grown often suffers badly from the depredations of flying foxes, of which there are swarms. During the mango season night watchmen are employed to make a noise by striking empty kerosene oil tins in order to frighten away these marauders.

The bananas and plantains looked good and tasted better. Papayas grow well too.

The mangoes I saw, though small, were of a golden colour and of excellent flavour, which resembled that of the famed Alphonso mango of Bombay. I heard later that these particular mangoes were grown from Alphonso grafts brought from Bombay.

To walk round the whole island of Male does not take long. At the eastern end of the island, and at no distance, lies the island of Hulele. From this point one sees the long line of barrier coral reef extending along the southern shore and hears the surf thundering over it. This would be a most suitable spot for the erection of a lighthouse.

Near by is a large shrine with white flags placed round it. The roof is thatched with *cadjan.* There are two tombs here, one that of a former sultan, the other of a very holy man or *pir* El Habshi which is Arabic for the negro.

It is related that the habshi was only a humble member of the crew of an Arab merchant dhow trading with the Maldives. It was seen, however, that when cargo was being discharged no pack or bale rested on his shoulders as with the others and that he had the power of levitation, never feeling therefore the weight of the burden. This was brought to the Sultan's ears, who immediately sent for the man as he thought he must be very saintly to be possessed of such powers.

The habshi was asked by the Sultan to stay at court and become a preceptor of religion to the people.

The roads from the south all lead to the centre of the town. They are all broad, straight and very well kept. There are several alleys leading off them which are apt to puzzle the stranger. Along the shore one passes several little groups of huts or villages which lie screened from the sea by groves of shady *suriya* trees, a species of hibiscus bearing a pale yellow flower and very common in Ceylon. At almost every place under the trees and quite near to the beach are rough benches forming a square and from many of the trees hang swings.

One of the places in fact resembled a kind of open-air club, for, in addition to the bench running along three sides of a square, there were rough chairs with backs and seats made of fine coir yarn. The village elders I suppose take their ease and gossip in the cool of the evening whilst the younger generation and the children amuse themselves with the swings. I saw several women sitting on the swings and one of them had a child in her arms. Others appeared intensely curious about me, peeping out from behind doors or fences. The women and children however disappeared within the moment I looked their way.

Further along, towards the south-west of Male,

can be seen the island of Viligili at no great distance. Further away are what look like green dots on the sea. These are other islands in the atoll. Seen at sunset the effect is particularly fine as the red glare of the setting sun lights up the foaming breakers on the south, and these distant *ra'* as the Maldivians call them—the Arab word for an island is *jazira*—and this word is invariably used by the crews of buggalows.

As darkness falls the islands gradually fade into the dark blue of the sea like a vanishing mirage.

It is interesting to note that the word atoll itself comes from the Maldives and I expect it was originally derived from the Sinhalese *aethule,* meaning within.

An atoll is the ring-shaped coral reef which encloses a lagoon in which there may or may not be islands.

At the extreme south-west of Male stands a small mosque, the Idu Miskit, to which the Sultan repairs in full State to proffer his prayers on the festival of *id-ul-fitr,* which immediately follows the fast of Ramadan similarly as Easter day follows Lent.

The plinth of the building is rather finely carved in coral lime stone which has become quite black with exposure; the workmanship and finish are distinctly good. The mosque itself, however, is not very old, having been built less than a century ago.

Skirting the coast can be seen a good portion of what once must have been the ramparts surrounding the town.

A considerable part of the old city wall still remains and at many places are gun emplacements and here and there some rusty old cannon. Some of these cannon I was told belonged originally to the Portuguese. Doubtless they have been several times in action and the ramparts have withstood many a siege and raid in the old forgotten past when unfriendly and covetous neighbours like the Malabar Moplahs and Portuguese came to loot and raid from the Maldivians, or, if possible, to possess themselves of the islands. The watchword of the Portuguese at that time was "Conquest, Commerce and Conversion", and they were evidently firm believers in the oft-quoted expression of "Trade follows the Flag".

The Maldives were held by the Portuguese from Goa for a period of ten years.

I learned subsequently from correspondence with His Excellency the Governor-General of Portuguese India, that there was no reference to this occupation in the official archives at Goa at the present time, and that all documents relative to this had been sent to Portugal in 1779.

Aliveira Martins in his book "Portugal on the Seas", and Denvers, "The Portuguese in India", both refer to the relations between Goa and the

1.

2

3.

4.

1. MALE ROADSTEAD
2. MAIDAN IN FRONT OF THE PALACE, MALÉ.
3. A ROAD IN MALÉ
4. THE MALL, IDHU MISKIT IN DISTANCE.

Maldive Islands, which were discovered by Dom Lourenco de Almeida in 1507.

The first reference is found in the Portuguese Chronicles, "The Lendas de India" and is cited by Yule and Burnell in Hobson Jobson. It reads:—

"But Dom Vasco .... said that things must go on as they were to India and there he would enquire into the truth. And so on arriving in the Gulf where the storm befell them, all were separated and that vessel which steered badly parted company with the fleet and found itself at one of the first islands of the Maldives, at which they stopped some days enjoying themselves, for the island abounded in provisions and the men indulged to excess in eating cocos and fish and drinking bad stagnant water and in disorders with women so that many died."

F. C. Denvers says in his work, "The Portuguese in India":—

"In 1646 the King of the Maldive Islands signed a treaty of vassalage with the King of Portugal.

"No copy of this treaty appears to have been preserved, but there is in existence a letter from the King of the Maldives dated 5th May, 1643, in which it is stated that under an agreement of former years he was bound to deliver to the Viceroy one-third of the coir fibre which he received as tribute."

R. S. Whiteáway in his book, "The Rise of Portuguese Power in India", 1547-1550, states:—

"Owing to the presence of Portuguese fleets on the Malabar coasts, the Mohammedan ships trading between the extreme east and the Red Sea, had taken a new route through the Maldives, that kept them clear of their enemies. The Viceroy despatched Dom Lourenco, his son, to close this route and to explore Ceylon, but owing to the ignorance of the pilots, he missed the Maldives though he reached Ceylon."

This happened some time between 1506 and 1507.

Francois Pyrard de Laval, whom I have referred to before, one of the survivors of the French ship "Corbin" which was wrecked in the Maldives in A.D. 1602, gives a graphic account of the Portuguese occupation and the events leading up to it. This occurred about fifty years previous to the date when he was shipwrecked and he learned about it during his sojourn of five years in the islands.

"About fifty years before this time (A.D. 1602) the King of these Islands (Sultan Hasan IX.) who was of noble and ancient lineage seeing that he was ill-obeyed and was unable to withstand a formidable rival who wished to depose him was inspired of God with a resolve to quit all.

"He departed secretely with his wife and some of his family, without saying a word of his destination to anyone and went straight to Cochin, where he became a Christian along with his wife and some of his followers, sending back such as would not be baptized. For this cause his rival who was his near relative was at once accepted as king. The name of the latter was Hali (Ali) of the other Assan (Hasan).

"This former King then, when he became a Christian at Cochin wrote word to all his subjects that they should become Christians and pay him their wonted tribute; otherwise he would come and see to it with a large army of Portuguese, who had promised him their aid. The new King and the Maldive people made answer that they would no longer acknowledge him; that if aught was due to him he might come and get it; that if he preferred to be a Christian he should remain where he was—as for them, they would sooner die than change their faith.

"Hearing this, he asked the aid of the Viceroy of the Indies at Goa; who promised it; but on terms that he should not go in person, as it was feared that he would not agree with his people, or might bring the Portuguese into difficulties.

"The Portuguese armed force set out, but was not able to effect anything, losing a galley with three ships, and a goodly number of men; and so were constrained to retire.

"The following year they returned with a stronger force and better pilots, and the new King went out bravely to meet them, though he knew himself lost; he might perhaps have escaped but he preferred to die in battle rather than to retreat with shame.

"He was vanquished and put to death, and the Portuguese made themselves masters of Male; where they built a Fortress and thence sallied forth to compel the submission of the other Islands, and put many of the inhabitants to the sword.

"Then they assembled all the Chiefs of the Islands and told them they desired to leave them at peace, and not to constrain them in any way, nor to change their religion, if only they would pay the (titular) King his dues.

"These terms being accepted, they left one of the Island Chiefs to govern, and to remain always at Male with the Portuguese Commandant; on terms that he should take no political measure but after consulting the Portuguese and the Island Chiefs, and that all the trade should be in the hands of the Portuguese alone.

"The Governor appointed by the Portuguese to rule under them as Viceroy was a Lord, a native of the Islands and of their religion; but he did everything in the name of the Christian king who lived in Portuguese territory.

"In this way the Portuguese ruled the Islands in peace for the space of ten years; during which time the father of this King (presently reigning,

Sultan Ibrahim III.) and his (the former's brother) were Catibes (Khatib) each of his own Island, but with the pride of their race would never submit to the Portuguese yoke, nor obey the Governor whom they had left in power.

"On the contrary, they rebelled and levied a force of men and galleys for war, and repaired to the Atallon (Atoll) Ouadou (huvadu) otherwise Souadou, at the southern extremity of the Islands, where the Portuguese dared not follow them, nor cross the Candou (M. Kadu) or Channel, of the said Atollon; so that neither this Atollon and the Islands belonging thereto nor any to the south of that Channel, were ever subject to the Portuguese.

"These two brothers then built a strong Fort, and being distant about eighty leagues from Male, where the Portuguese were, they became in time so strong in men, arms, and ammunition, that they, as it were held, Male and the Portuguese in check, so that they durst not come out without daily experiencing a harassing war.

"This lasted for eight years, at the end of which arrived four galleys of Malabar corsairs for the purpose of war and pillage, as was their wont. The two brothers accosted them, and agreed with them to make war upon the Portuguese on terms of half the booty.

"So one day, getting word that the Captain of the Fortress and Island of Male was gone to

Cochin with a goodly number of Portuguese soldiers, they could not miss the opportunity, and resolved to attack the Fortress; which project they carried out so well, that one night they surprised it by escalade, and made themselves masters of the place, putting to death upwards of three hundred men that were within, and taking prisoner the Native Governor who was set there by the Portuguese.

"The place being taken and sacked, the Malabars, having got their agreed share of the spoil were going home, and leaving the two brothers masters of the town; but they were jealous to see so much of the riches of the Islands being carried off, and resolved to attack the Malabars. This they did, and, after a long engagement at length were left victorious, and got both the booty and the galleys, sending the men back to the Malabar coast and thus repaid with treachery the good services they had of them.

"In this manner the two brothers became kings of the Islands, and equally shared the throne without any quarrel between them. They were both men of great valour and were acknowledged as such by the people.

"As for the Portuguese, they were indignant at the rebuff they had received at the Maldives and were resolved to avenge it; so the next year they sent an army to the Islands, and carried on the war for a long time; but the two Kings defeated all their forces. This war lasted three years.

"These Kings were very powerful, and possessed two Fortresses, that of Male and the other at the Atoll of Souadou, or Ouadou, in an Island called Game.

"At length both parties considered that it would be for the good of the country and of trade to come to some sort of understanding rather than to continue this war to a doubtful issue.

"Accordingly they made a Treaty with these conditions, viz., that the Maldive Kings and their people should be left in peace to possess the Islands in like manner as their predecessors, save that they should give a certain pension to their Christian King, his successors, and heirs, to be rendered at Cochin, but without acknowledging him in any other way; on the other hand, the Mohometan Kings at the Islands should not be allowed to take the title and name of King though they were to be absolute in all things, but only that of Prince, Duke, or the like; also, that those two brothers only should be entitled to this name, in their language Quilague (M. Kilege), and that they should be responsible for the payment of the pension of the Christian King, who, on his part was allowed to have a Factor there.

"Furthermore, all natives of the Maldives desiring to traffic with other countries, were bound to take a passport from the Portuguese; as were all the other Indians that were at peace with them."

Such were the terms of this Peace, which has endured to the present day (A.D. 1619).

Pyrard writing in A.D. 1618 states:—

"I have heard it said by the islanders that the trade and prosperity of the islands were never so great as when the Portuguese governed there."

The account in the "Tarikh" (Arab History) or "Chronicle of the Sultans of the Maldive Islands", of the Portuguese seizure and occupation of Male is thus given by Bell who examined and edited the existing copy in 1920 and 1922, and states that its language and character are Arabic:—

"The important events recorded by Pyrard, on the strength of oral tradition, appear set down by the compiler of the 'Tarikh' with an unsophisticated charm, not free of that quaint romance and fervent religious tone so marked throughout this valuable, if strangely uneven, Muslim Chronicle.

"A.D. 1550. When Sultan Muhammad had reigned for two years and four months, his brother Hasan seized the throne, after murdering him. Having ruled for two years and five months, he determined to change his religion, and proclaimed his intention publicly in the 959th year of the Hijra. He then departed for Cochin, where he embraced the Infidels' Faith, and even adopted their mode of dress. After residing there for two years, he went to Goa; where, some time afterwards, he married a Christian lady of good birth, by whom he had several children.

"A.D. 1554-56. At the Maldives Abu Bakr (II) son of Ibrahim Farina Kilegefanu ascended the throne after a while. The name of his mother was Sanfa Diyo. He reigned for four months, and died a martyr's death in Hijra 962.

"A.D. 1557-58. He was succeeded by 'Ali (VI), son of 'Abd-ur-Rahman, Prime Minister. His mother's name was Sitti Kabadi Kilege of Feridu (Island, Ari Atoll). Ten months later he was killed in battle with the Christians.

"Know the origin of this war.

"The Sultan Hasan, who had become a Christian, desiring to convert the Maldivian Ministers and Chiefs, sent a Portuguese vessel to bring them to Cochin. On arrival at Male, the Captain of the vessel informed the Ministers, etc., that he had come there to remove them to Cochin at the request of their Sultan. The inhabitants held a meeting and decided not to go, or obey the orders of their Infidel Ruler. Then they fought the invaders, killing all of them, and seized their goods. Those who took part in the fighting against these invaders were the aforesaid Sultans Abu Bakr II. and 'Ali VI. with their supporters. All this took place before they came to the throne. Again those (the Portuguese) at Cochin sent a fresh force, which also was defeated, and all slain by the Maldivians, who seized the ship with its entire cargo and arms. For the third time a force, fully armed, was conveyed in a great fleet to Male, under the command of Captain Andiri Andiri. Sultan 'Ali had then been on the throne for two months and fifteen days.

"A.D. 1558. The enemy landed one night on the west beach of Male with their cannon. Thereupon Sultan 'Ali accompanied by his soldiers, armed with swords, lances, bows and arrows, sallied forth to oppose the invaders. The Sultan, bearing sword and shield, marched at the head of his soldiers. He had gone as far as the Id Mosque when he found that the soldiers had all deserted him, with the exception of the Prime Minister and his personal attendant—the only two that remained with him. Then these three warriors, facing the enemy, charged them with the courage of lions. The foe astounded at their bravery ceased advancing, and, terror-stricken, began to fire on them from a distance, until they had killed all three. Then without much resistance, they (the Portuguese) seized the Kingdom.

"Sultan 'Ali died in Hijra 965 A.D. 1558 at the end of the month Sh' Aban and Andiri Andiri ascended the throne. God knoweth better than we men what happened at that time."

In A.D. 1573 Muhammad Khatib Takurufanu who subsequently became Sultan under the name of Muhammad Khatib Takurufanu the Great, launched a surprise attack on the Portuguese garrison in Male, "when the Christians were making merry with song and carousal", and after some desperate fighting the Portuguese were practically annihilated and Male was wrested from the rule of the hated *farangi*.

The Tarikh thus comments on the Maldivian victory:—

"The calamity, fear and sorrow which the Portuguese suffered were sympathized in neither by Heaven nor Earth, which wept not for them. Their rule and power proved as transcient as sunbeams. Their name was detested by the people and their might had departed forever."

In A.D. 1631 in the reign of Sultan Muhammad Imad-ud-din the Portuguese again attacked Male but they were driven back with great loss.

> "God filled the hearts of the foe with fear so that they fled from Male terror-stricken"

piously affirms the chronicler of the Tarikh.

Once more in A.D. 1650 the Portuguese made another attempt to capture Male (this was in the reign of Sultan Iskandar Ibrahim I.), but were again repulsed and suffered defeat at the hands of the Maldivians and were forced to withdraw.

> "God granted the Maldivians the victory over their enemy and the Portugese had not the courage to come again to the Maldives"

to quote again the Tarikh.

The Tribute which had been previously paid to the Portuguese for many years was stopped.

The independence of the Maldives was thus gained and the Sultan Iskandar Ibrahim I. was acknowledged as a great ruler.

Towards the end of the seventeenth century, with the gradual decline of the Portuguese power in Eastern seas and the rise of the Dutch the former found their trade harassed by the latter. As the power of the Dutch increased in India, Ceylon and the islands farther east, the Portuguese were gradually ousted from almost all their eastern territories. But not only was the Portuguese Eastern trade harassed by the Dutch, but also in lesser degree by the English and French.

There is a very interesting document which bears on the situation in the Maldives during part of the period of the Dutch rule in Ceylon.

This is a memorandum of instructions left by Governor J. G. Loten for his successor Jan Schreuder, and is dated the 28th February, 1757. It has been translated from the Dutch by Mr. E. Reimers, the official Archivist to the Government of Ceylon, to whom I am indebted for a copy of the translation which I give below:—

" Regarding the Maldive Islands, the Heer van Gollenesse has made all the necessary observations; and as he has made reference to Their Excellencies' Order not to pay more for a cotty of Cowries (that is 25 lbs.) than two rix-dollars, which according to an order received later by letters of August 31, 1753, was reduced to one and a half rix-dollars. I have nothing further to add to this except that the Maldivians still come quite willingly in their little boats to trade with us notwithstanding the reduced rates.

"But regarding the present position of the government in these islands, I should like to add here that towards the latter part of 1753 a letter arrived by the Sultan's vessel from his court dignitaries by which they informed us that their Sultan had been taken by force and carried to another place through the treachery of his prime minister and the people of one Ali Raja of Cannanore, who, as we were informed later, was the king of that country, but that thereupon the people had cast that minister of state into the sea and had themselves assumed control of the government, which domination having become very tyrannical and insupportable for the court dignitaries and the legitimate Maldivian subjects, one night, when their tyrants were not suspecting any such thing, they massacred all of them with the latter's own weapons, and again took possession of the Maldive Islands.

"The envoy who brought the above-mentioned letter from the court dignitaries, at the same time requested that he might be supplied with some munitions of war and provisions, but he was granted only six lasts of rice and some timber for payment in cash.

"Scarcely a year later, a letter was again received through the Maldive envoy addressed to us by order of the abducted Maldive Sultan's daughter now reigning over the Maldive Islands, by the second in authority in that island, and at the same time French letter signed by one Le Termellier the latter of which contained a request for our assistance for purchasing some provisions and also informed us that he had planted the French flag on the Maldive Islands because Monseigneur the Marquis (meaning Monsieur du Pleix) had granted his protection to those lands.

"In the following year, that is to say up to the end of 1755, no further letters were received, but vessels arrived both here and at Galle and Tutucorin which sold their cowries to the Company at the ordinary rates and also brought us the information that the King had not yet returned and that his daughter continued to reign.

"In like manner a letter was recently received in November addressed to us by the same regent in which nothing was stated about the daughter's reign; but from a statement obtained by us on the 18th November, 1756, it appears that the government still continues in the daughter's name and also that the King of Cannanore had written a letter to the Maldives requesting that four distinguished persons might be sent to reconduct the abducted Sultan back to his country; and for the rest, the Maldive informants confirmed the full report sent to us by the Councillors of the abducted King on September 15, 1753, adding that the regent of whom we have already spoken, and who was in charge of the direction of affairs until the King's return, had taken into his service Frenchmen for his own security and in order to restrain the people."

The Ali Raja of Cannonore mentioned in the Governor's memorandum bore the inherited title of the "Sea King". He took Male in A.D. 1752 and deported the Sultan Muhammad Mukarram Imad-ud-din III., who subsequently died in exile at Minicoy (Maliku) in the Lacadives.

CHAPTER IV

MALDIVE FISH

THE early mornings and afternoons and evenings are of course the best times for walking. The noon-day heat is usually very great, especially if the wind has dropped. The white sandy roads, too, are trying to the eyes on account of the glare they occasion. During this part of the day it is better to keep indoors and exert oneself as little as possible.

On another day I paid a second visit to the Indian merchants and found them busy weighing dried fish which had just been brought in. The normal method of exchange is for the merchant to give four bags of rice, each bag containing two and a half bushels, and weighing approximately one hundred and sixty pounds, for one and three-quarter cwt. of dried Maldive fish. The Maldivian Government impose a duty of one bag in every twelve on the imported rice and similarly with regard to kerosene oil, one tin in every twelve. The freight by buggalow from Colombo is one rupee per bag of rice. The price of rice varies of course but its value is always taken as the standard and calculations made accordingly. The value of the rice is comparatively low as compared with that of the dried fish generally called Maldive fish. This commands a ready market in Ceylon at remunerative prices. It is highly esteemed by the Sinhalese who call it *umbalakada,* and it is largely used by them as a condiment. The Maldivian word for it is *kalubila mas* or *kadu mas.*

Before use the hard, dried fish, which is in pieces of six to eight inches in length, is scraped and whittled down to small fragments. To this is added onions or spices. It is then cooked and served as an adjunct to curry and rice or for even rice without curry for those who cannot always afford to eat curry.

The value of the annual export of Maldive fish to Ceylon is well above £200,000, and Bell in his Sessional Paper, "Report on a visit to Male, 1921", states that the striking growth in the importation of this commodity into Ceylon amounts to very nearly 1,500 per cent. during the past sixty years.

It can thus be easily understood that the Borah merchants are able to turn over a very handsome profit on their transactions. They have the added advantage of knowing the current market price both of rice and Maldive fish from the latest arrived buggalow and can therefore base their calculations to allow of a good margin of profit, whereas the islander is entirely ignorant of such prices and has perforce to accept the dictum of the merchants.

It so happens sometimes that the Maldivian is unable to take away with him the full amount of rice which is his due as an *odi* cannot as a rule load more than two hundred bags. In this case he leaves the balance of rice due him to be called for later and accepts a note from the merchant that the balance of rice still due will be handed over whenever required.

The islander may not return for months to claim his due, or he may die or be drowned, in which latter case the claim is made by his inheritor, but the latter has to produce the note in court and prove it.

If the Maldivian Government were to erect a wireless receiving station and arrange that once a week the market prices of rice and Maldive fish were broadcasted from Colombo it would enable the simple islanders to have a clearer idea of their relative value and possibly obtain better prices for their fish.

I understand that the question of establishing a wireless station at Male has of late years been under the consideration of the Maldivian Government, but it is not yet *un fait accompli*. The islands lying so low, and with nothing intervening, reception should be particularly good from Ceylon.

It is said that the first Borah merchant in Ceylon to establish trade relations with the

Maldives, nearly a century ago, was Allibhoy Essajee. I understand, too, he was also the first Borah to land in Ceylon and embark on business. It was in Galle that he first traded and later moved to Colombo. His nephew, the late Carimjee Jafferjee, was a worthy successor to him. He developed the Maldivian trade which his uncle had initiated, having a fleet of seven buggalows and a schooner. He died honoured and respected and loved by the Ceylonese for his probity, generosity and public spirit. The firm carried on by his descendants still flourishes in Colombo.

It was not very long before other Borah merchants followed in the wake of Essajee and Jafferjee, and opened warehouses and shops in Male with their representatives. The Maldivian trade can be said to be entirely in the hands of the Borahs, and has been a source of considerable profit to them. They take risks of course with their buggalows as these vessels have no *bima* or insurance, nor has the cargo which they carry, and occasionally ship and cargo are lost in bad weather.

As regards the fishing industry as carried on in the Maldives, which forms the chief industry of the Archipelago, it may be interesting to note that the fish is of the tunny or bonito species and is rather handsome in appearance. It is of a dark blue colour down the back, the rest of the body being a shimmering silvery white rather like the sheen of a mackerel. There are no scales on the body and when the fish is cut open the flesh is quite red, rather resembling raw beef in colour. As previously mentioned it is called *kalubila mas* by the Maldivians and is known to the Sinhalese as *khelawella.*

Eight, ten or more fishermen go out in a *mas-odi,* the larger type of fishing boat. The smaller type or *mas-dhoni* is manned by four to six men. In sunny weather the fishermen wear a peculiar coal-scuttle-shaped hat, rather after the style of an early Victorian bonnet, only that the shade comes well over the eyes as a protection from the glare of the water. The hat is made of fine matting inside and is covered with quilted cotton cloth after the manner of an Indian pig-sticker helmet.

The colour of the cloth is in accordance with the fancy of the wearer, some are pink, whilst others are green or blue. They are very light and afford excellent protection from the glare. Before going far out to sea the men first contrive to catch with a net as many as possible of a small fish of the sardine variety. These are thrown into the bottom of the boat where a quantity of water has been previously left for them. When a sufficiently large number have been obtained, sea-cocks are opened and the quantity of water increased and freshened to keep the fish alive. Often a boat is almost down to the gunwale. The vessel then proceeds under sail to the open sea, sometimes twelve or fifteen miles out.

The fishermen watch where any gulls appear to be hovering over a particular spot and make for this place as they know there must be fish about. Having arrived at the place one of the crew proceeds to throw out handfuls of the small fish into the sea as ground bait. If the larger fish are on the feed they immediately begin to swarm around the boat. Then is the fisherman's opportunity.

Each man, four to six of them on either side of the boat, stands ready with a rod and short line. They at once cast their lines and hooks into the water. These hooks are not baited nor have they any 'barb like the usual fish-hook. They are almost crescent in shape but somewhat flattened out in the centre and about three inches in length. They are tinned over and in the water their mimicry of a small sardine is wonderful. The hooks are cast simultaneously with the throwing in of the small fish and are at once snapped at by the swarming fish. As a fish is hooked the fisherman, with a facility and adroitness which comes of long practice, whips the fish out with the rod and swings it over his shoulder and into the boat. There being no barb, the fish automatically drops into the part of the boat which is separated from where the small fish are kept. The fisherman proceeds to cast again immediately.

I was told that when fish are really on the rise they are caught so rapidly in this manner that in a very short space of time five hundred or even as many as a thousand fish are caught and deposited in the boat. The fish are not the very large tunny and range from about three to ten lbs. in weight.

It so happens that sometimes the fish suddenly leave the place and proceed elsewhere, in which case the fishermen have again to go in search of their whereabouts, often a long and arduous business. Sometimes no fish whatever are caught, or, perhaps, only a very few and the boats return home often after a fruitless voyage.

When the fish are brought in they are cut up into four, six, or eight pieces, according to their size, and the head and vertebra removed. The pieces are then put in caldrons containing a mixture of fresh and salt water and boiled, and when this water becomes thick and turns dark brown it is called *rihakuru.* The oil rising to the surface is skimmed off and kept for smearing on the outside of the boats to preserve the wood and keep the seams water-tight. After boiling, the pieces are placed in layers on open racks made of bamboos under which a fire made of coconut husks is burning. In this manner they are gradually smoked and dried and after some days when the process is completed they are ready for the market.

The life of the Maldivian fisherman like the life of all fishermen is precarious. Sometimes the fishing boats through sudden storms or stress of weather are blown far out of their course and it is with difficulty they find their way back to harbour. Sometimes, of course, they never return. Not so long ago the crew of a Maldivian sailing craft underwent a terrible ordeal at sea.

An account of their experience appeared in the Ceylon Press, and I give it as showing some of the dangers these intrepid men have to face.

"The Maldivians left Male in the month of July en route for one of the other islands of the group. While crossing the Karadivu channel they encountered a severe gale and were tossed about badly. The men did everything possible to put back to Male but the adverse winds drove them further out to sea. For four days they made heroic efforts to return to Male or to put in to any of the islands where they could remain in shelter, but the storm raged with such fury the more precarious their position became as they drifted further and further out to the open sea. To add further to their troubles the supply of water ran out.

"On the fifth day the Dutch steamer 'Royal' picked up the men who were taken on board and cared for.

Most of the men, however, who are in charge of the boats have a very good working knowledge of navigation. There are several small schools of navigation in Male in which experienced men of the community teach the use of a compass and other nautical instruments.

The intrepidity of the Maldivians as mariners is thus aptly described by Pyrard.

"The natives have a wonderful dexterity in avoiding dangerous places. I have seen them sail so nicely as to rub upon rocks on both sides without any damage. Both the rich and the poor are inured to the sea from their infancy and fear not to encounter the most turbulent and foaming seas in little boats and barks, the number of which is unaccountable, for the poorest man that is has one and the rich have several.

"Travelling under their conduct I suffered the gravest apprehensions but I was never so afraid as on one occasion when I was with some of them in a little boat of not more than four arm lengths, in a sea towering above me two pikes high. Every moment it seemed that a wave would carry me off the boat, wherein I had much trouble to hold myself, whilst they recked nothing of it and only laughed.

"The greatest part of the islands comprehended in one Attollon are surrounded with a common flat or bar that is only possible at one or two narrow places which are not easily observed and for that reason it is necessary for them to be very expert in the management of their boats or barks since the least slip is certainly followed with shipwreck and the loss of their goods; as for their own persons indeed they have no great reason to fear for all of them swim admirably well.

" Notwithstanding that wonderful dexterity in sailing they frequently lose their barks which is occasioned by the currents called *oyivarus* which run east and west six months upon the east coast and six months upon the west, but with such uncertainty that the change happens sooner or later at one time than another."

CHAPTER V

THE TRIBUTE. FRIDAY PRAYERS

THE name given to the Maldivians by the Indian merchants and the crews of the buggalows is *kaliya*. This, however, is considered rather derogatory by the inhabitants. It is derived from the Maldivian word *kalo*, meaning thou, and from the habit of the natives in addressing each other in this manner the word has been corrupted to *kaliya*.

The correct word for a Maldivian in their language is *divessei*—a man of the islands—*dwipa* is the Sanskrit and *dhuva* the Sinhalese for an island. The Maldivians call the Maldives *Divehi Raje*—the kingdom of islands.

Bell states that the ancient name for Male was Mafacalou or "Sultan's Island", and that the word Maldive is derived from the complex Mahal Palace, and Diva Island, and Male has given its appelation to the entire Maldive Archipelago. Ibn Batuta, the Arab voyager of the fourteenth century, gives "Mahal" the principal island, "the province after which all the islands are called"

Ceylon itself was known to the Arabs as Serendib, Seren probably being a corruption of Sinhala. In fact the name of Sinhaldip is still used by many of the Indian crews of buggalows.

The present ruler of the Maldives is Sultan Muhammad Shams-ud-Din Iskandar III. The Sultans of the Maldives have been possessed of absolute powers for a period of over eight hundred years. The Government when I visited Male was carried on by a Bodu Wazir or Prime Minister who was also the Chief Treasurer, the Qazi or Chief Justice and Naibus or Magistrates besides other officers of state who looked after such matters as the customs, post office, police and revenue.

Subsequently and as recently as 1932 on the 22nd of December in that year the Sultan renounced his prerogatives and granted a constitution to the people on more or less democratic lines at a durbar held on that date. I understand that the new constitution was introduced at the express desire of the Sultan himself. I shall refer more fully to this subject later on.

The coins in use and accepted as legal tender are the Indian silver rupee, the Indian eight anna and four anna pieces, and coins of the corresponding value in Ceylon currency. Paper money is not as a rule accepted. The local money is a small, rough-shaped copper coin with Arabic characters on it called a *lari*. One hundred and twenty of these are equivalent to a rupee. A slightly larger copper coin equivalent to four *lari* is called a *bodulari,* which means a big *lari.*

Recently *laris* have been minted in England for the Maldivian Government. These are remarkably well made and a great improvement on the old *lari.* The inscription on the older *laris* and *bodularis* set forth the title of the Sultan as *Sultan nul Barru wal Bahuru,* "King of Land and Sea". On the newer coinage this has been omitted and only the Sultan's name is inscribed. The Government issues its own stamps and these all bear the picture of the minaret of the Great Mosque. They are of the value of 2, 3, and 10 cents respectively.

It is curious to find that the numerals in the Maldivian language up to and including twelve are practically the same as in Sinhalese. From thirteen upwards Hindustani words are used with very slight variations.

The days of the week are a mixture of Sinhalese, Hindustani and Maldivian. The use of Hindustani words is undoubtedly due to the Maldive trade with India which has been in existence for centuries. Practically all the Maldivian officials are conversant with Hindustani and all those whom I met spoke it quite fluently. A large number of the people are able to read and write Arabic, which is taught in the schools by the Khatibs or priests of the Mosques.

THE TRIBUTE

The Government of Ceylon exercises a suzerainty over the Maldive islands and in recognition of this the Sultan pays an annual tribute to the Governor of Ceylon. There is, however, no interference whatsoever by the Ceylon Government with regard to the government of the country or its laws, traditions and customs of the people. The Maldivians being a peaceable and law-abiding people desire nothing so much as to be left alone to manage their affairs in their own way.

With regard to the tribute itself, this is not a payment in money, but consists of gifts of rolls of the finest Maldivian mats, beautiful lacquer work, Maldivian sweetmeats made from powdered rice and coconut palm honey, known as *bondi-halua,* a pungent fish preparation called *rihakuru,* in large earthenware jars, shells of many varieties, and a small quantity of ambergris.

The Sultan's state schooner, the "Fath-ul-Majid", bearing these gifts usually arrives in Colombo some time in November, synchronizing with the finish of the south-west monsoon.

An afternoon is fixed for the presentation and the schooner gaily dressed with flags for the occasion is boarded by the Maldivian Representative, who after a short while returns to the jetty accompanied by several *divahin.* They are met by the Ceylon Lascoreen Guard in their picturesque uniform of a bygone day, a long red coat with gold facings, white cotton trousers, and curious shaped helmets. They have their band as well, consisting of large native drums and a species of clarinet.

Some Ceylonese officials in uniform and gold lace are likewise in attendance.

A detachment of the Ceylon police looking very smart in their dark blue uniforms and armed with rifles is also present.

A procession is formed with the Maldivian Representative at the head of it. He wears a flowing black Arab *jelab* and a white turban and an attendant holds an umbrella over him. The Lascoreen Guard and their band lend a distinctly old-world touch, their gay uniforms making a contrast with the more sombre tone of the police.

The procession then proceeds on foot to Queen's House, the residence of the Governor, to the accompaniment of a barbaric march played by the band of the Lascoreen Guard.

In the rear of the procession are Maldivian stalwarts bearing the various gifts composing the tribute on their heads.

The streets through which the procession passes are lined with sightseers, for the ceremony is quite unique in its way. Many Ceylonese come from long distances to see it.

In the windows of the Grand Oriental Hotel and those of offices and shops on the route many European spectators can also be seen.

(*Upper*) PROCESSION WITH MALDIVIAN TRIBUTE, CEYLON.

(*Lower*) PROCESSION OF SULTAN TO IDHU MISKIT AFTER RAMADAN.

Arrived at Queen's House the Maldivian Representative is received in state by the Governor and some of his senior officials, both European and Ceylonese.

An exchange of compliments takes place and the Maldivian Representative presents a letter wrapped in silk as is customary in the East, addressed by the Sultan to the Governor. It is interesting to add that when the presentation of the letter takes place, although the Maldivian Representative is perfectly acquainted with English, the conversation is carried on through two interpreters. The Governor speaks in English and this is translated by a Tamil-speaking interpreter into Tamil to the Maldivian interpreter who understands Tamil, and he in turn translates from Tamil into Maldivian to the Maldivian Representative and the reply of the latter to the Governor also goes through the same channel. The tribute is thereafter handed over to and duly acknowledged by the Governor.

Then there is a further exchange of compliments followed possibly by tea. After this, the Maldivian Representative formally takes his leave and the function is over for another year.

The Ceylon Government in return sends a letter to the Sultan accompanied by some of the products of Ceylon, such as cinnamon, cardamoms, engraved Sinhalese brass-ware, etc.

With regard to ambergris, this resinous and

wax-like substance is largely used by manufacturers of high-priced perfumery and, in fact, forms the base of many scents. Formerly it was also used in cookery. It is highly esteemed among the Arabs who sometimes employ an extract of it to scent coffee on special occasions or use small quantities as incense and also of course as a perfume. It commands a very high price in both oriental and occidental countries being a substance which is comparatively rare. It is said to be vomited by the sperm whale from its intestines and is found in tropical seas, either floating on the water as it is very light, or washed up on the beach in small or large lumps.

Ambergris is found occasionally on the shores of the different islands of the Maldivian Archipelago by the inhabitants. Being a monopoly of the Government it is all brought in to the Government stores at Male where it is kept and later sold principally in Bombay. In Pyrard's time, theft or concealment of ambergris was punished with decapitation. The ambergris found in the Maldives is reputed to be the finest in the world. It is graded in the Government stores into three qualities. The first grade is whitish-grey in colour, the second is a dark brown, whilst the third and lowest is almost black.

Shortly before the advent of the state schooner and towards the end of the south-west monsoon the harbour of Colombo is invaded by several

Maldivian craft which have taken advantage of the favourable wind, and when the force of the monsoon is nearly spent to voyage to Colombo.

They bring the usual exports of dried fish, copra, and coir yarn which are disposed of and with the money thus obtained they purchase their requirements of food-stuffs, cloth, and other articles in Colombo.

These boats usually stay in port for some months waiting till the north-east monsoon is well advanced and return to their island homes with the favourable wind. During their stay in port the crews can be frequently met with in the streets and bazaars of Colombo.

To their unsophisticated eyes it is indeed a wonder city and they never seem tired of gazing into the shop windows. In some of the shops in Male, European patent medicines are sold, but at the time of my visit there was no actual Government dispensary or hospital of any kind, the inhabitants depending chiefly on *hakimi* drugs, and medicines which in many cases are empirical though one is told of some miraculous cures being effected. Doubtless the element of faith enters largely into this. There was at that time no qualified practitioner or surgeon so that no operations as understood by us could possibly be carried out.

In cases of accident and injury, indigenous drugs are employed and it is probably a case of kill or cure and I imagine much depends on the actual power of resistance in the patient, as any knowledge of aseptic conditions is non-existent.

Whilst I was in Male I heard that a young man, a relative of the Sultan, had only just returned from Colombo where he had been for an operation on his ear.

Pyrard thus describes the art of healing obtaining in his time in the Maldives and I have no doubt matters have changed very little since then in this respect.

"In all external inflammations or aches they apply fire which raises a scar and upon that they lay cotton dipped in coconut oil which cures them. Their ulcers which are very frequent among them, especially on the legs, are cured by laying plates of copper on them which do it effectually. Besides the remedies here mentioned they have some receipts and compositions of their herbs and drugs for several diseases, and especially for wounds at curing of which they are dexterous enough and yet they know not the use of lint or bandage for they only apply ointments.

"They are sometimes troubled with catarrhs, defluxions and pains in the bones. Venereal diseases are frequent among them; however, they cure them with china-wood (China radix).

"They are altogether unacquainted with the toothache which they owe to continual chewing of betel, for that fortifies the gums."

Skin diseases, too, are prevalent, but they cure these by applying indigenous medicinal oils.

Many suffer from blindness and sore eyes. Some, too, are afflicted with night bimdness, probably caused by the intense glare from the sea and the white coral sand.

I understand, however, that the Maldivian Government has now established a dispensary and engaged the services of a qualified medical practitioner from Ceylon. It must, however, be a difficult matter to induce a medical man who is not actually a Maldivian himself to stay permanently in the Maldives unless the salary and emoluments are particularly attractive.

There is no reason why if the Maldivian Government wish to be progressive a few promising young men from the community should not be sent either to India or Ceylon or even to Europe to study and become proficient in the art and science of medicine or surgery, and minister to the needs of the people.

There seemed to me to be a reluctance on the part of the Sultan's government to encourage their young men to study abroad. I surmised the real reason for this was not so much the lack of a desire to be progressive as the lurking fear that these young men would some day return and having, perhaps, imbibed democratic or socialistic ideas when pursuing their studies, might seek to instil these into the minds of the people and thus possibly prove a source of embarrassment and trouble to the age-old conservative order of things.

I landed in Male on a Monday, and on the Friday following I went to see the Sultan's procession returning from the Jama Masjid after prayers. Friday among Moslems is observed in the same manner as Sunday with Christians and the first portion of the day is reserved for prayer.

I left the house about one o'clock as I was told that prayers would finish about half-past one. The streets seemed quite deserted and silent and every shop and little boutique was closed.

The whole atmosphere reminded me of nothing so much as a small township or village in the north of Scotland on a Sunday. This effect was further heightened by the fact that it was a dull grey day with heavy rain clouds working up from the south-west.

I posted myself at a corner near the high walled palace of the Sultan which commanded a good view of the approach to the mosque. After a time two men with reddish check turbans, bare to the waist and wearing dark brown sarongs with two broad stripes at the foot and edged with white strolled past. These I was told were the nucleus of the band and some had gone to fetch the drums. Later a figure all in white wearing a long flowing Arab *jibbah* and white turban walked past in a stately manner. This was the Khatib or High Priest himself who had just finished prayers. Except for the turban he might have been the photographic negative of a Scotch Minister leaving the kirk without doffing his black Geneva gown. The Mullah even wore what appeared very like a round starched collar which closely resembled the regulation ecclesiastical "dog collar". He was followed by another white-robed figure carrying a parcel wrapped in a dark silk cloth which contained the Koran Sharif and other devotional books. Then appeared some men in white coats or blouses edged with black, with black shoulder straps and black piping on the sleeves. On the head was a small red cap attached to a light chain. These were members of the Police Force or Civil Guard.

Shortly after, about forty of the Sultan's *lashkar* or Guards lined up on either side of the road, the leader or colour-sergeant bearing a white furled flag. They all wore check turbans, were bare to the waist and wore the same kind of sarong as the bandsmen, only the colour was dark blue instead of brown. Half of them were armed with lances and the remainder with what looked like very ancient muzzle loaders.

In the waist cloth of each could be seen the ivory handle, in some cases mounted in silver work, of a dagger much resembling an Arab *jambir,* or Persian *khanjar.* The sheaths had ornamental silk tassels at the tip. There was a fanfare of trumpets which heralded the trumpeters with long brass instruments. They were immediately followed by two men with what are known on the Indian frontier as a *saranai*—a kind of clarinet. The moment the trumpets ceased the clarinets burst forth in a weird minor strain. They were accompanied by three drummers, each bearing what is called in India a *dhol* or large drum and a *beru* by the Maldivians. This is beaten with both hands.

Then came a young man, the nephew of the Sultan, who represented him. Close behind and on either side of him were two umbrella bearers. One of the umbrellas was the white State one used only by the Sultan or his representative, whilst the other was of a delicate rose colour. Both had gilded tops and were elaborately frilled.

The young man wore over a *jibbah* of dark green a *saduriya* or waistcoat of salmon colour and had a tarbush on his head. He looked neither to his right nor his left but straight ahead and passed through the gateway leading to the palace.

The Sultan does not himself always attend Friday prayers, and on this occasion neither the Prince nor the Prime Minister were present as both were indisposed.

The last I saw of the procession as it disappeared through the gate was the umbrellas being twirled around rapidly over the representative's head.

Except on the occasions of religious festivals, Friday is the only day during the week that the Sultan chooses to leave his palace. He leads, I believe, a very secluded life.

I wonder he does not sometimes find it boring to live in this manner as I should imagine the amusements and pastimes he may have to relieve the tedium and monotony of his life must be very limited.

I was disappointed with the physique of the Sultan's *lashkar* which with one or two exceptions seemed poor, and their ages varied greatly. The men of the Civil Guard were much better built and stronger looking.

One morning after I had spent some days in Male a public announcement was made as is usual in such cases by beat of drum. It was to the effect that for three days all the male inhabitants, both men and boys, unless excused for valid reasons, should work on repairs to the breakwater. This is Government work and such annual repairs are very necessary to prevent the erosion likely to be caused by heavy seas during the south-west monsoon. Every able-bodied male is expected to give his labour free for the general benefit of the community. It is in fact a kind of corvee imposed by the Government.

A similar system existed I believe in Ceylon under the name of Rajakariar, but was abolished about 1832.

In consequence of the order, all government offices and shops were closed to allow of the inhabitants carrying out their allotted share of the labour. No one appeared to object, and, in fact, everybody seemed quite cheerful over the work, recognizing it to be one of necessity and therefore requiring to be done. There are large stacks of coral everywhere and these are used principally for building and repair work.

Next in importance to the dried-fish industry is coir making. The coir of the Maldives has been known for centuries for its light colour, fineness and strength. It is said that the Portuguese in former times obtained most of the rope required by their fleets in the Indies from the Maldives.

Coconuts and coir are exported chiefly to India, very little going to Ceylon.

A large quantity of tortoise-shell is exported to Ceylon, the annual value of this product amounting to over £3,000. Pyrard states that " the Maldivy Tortoise Shells are much valued as being uncommon . . . being very beautiful, smooth, black, and full of fine natural figures ".

I heard incidentally that in certain places pearl oysters had been found containing pearls of good size and lustre, but there was a good deal of reticence about this, presumably because if the fact became generally known it might excite the cupidity of foreigners and lead to a demand for concessions and exploitation.

The number of sea shells found in these islands is extraordinary as is also the beauty of their shapes and variety of colouring. This is in considerable contrast to the coast of Ceylon where very few shells of any size or quality are to be seen on the shore. There are fine "Triton" shells, some of very large size, beautifully marked outside in dark and light brown, the inner portion being of a delicate pink. There are numerous other kinds, some spotted, some dark brown, some quite white, down to the humble cowrie shell, which last till quite recently was used in Bengal chiefly as a form of currency and is still much in demand for ornamentation.

The collecting of cowries for export forms an industry in itself.

Pyrard in referring to cowries writes:—

"They send also little shells that contain a creature in them of the bigness of the end of one's little finger, white, very smooth and glittering .... These go only to Bengal, the inhabitants of which esteem them so much that I have seen thirty or forty ships laden without any other commodity bound thither, though in Bengal they have gold and silver and plenty of other metals, yet these shells pass there as money and the king and noblemen hoard up prodigious quantities of them accounting them their treasure . . ."

There is also reference to the trade in cowrie shells by Ibn Batuta, the Arab traveller of the fourteenth century, and is thus described by him:—

"The money of the Islanders (of the Maldives) consists of cowries (al-wada). They so style creatures which they collect in the sea, and bury in holes dug on the shore. The flesh wastes away, and only a white shell remains. Hundred of these shells are called 'Siyah' and 700 'fal'; 12,000 are called 'Kutta'; and 100,000 'bustu'. Bargains are made with these cowries at the rate of 4 'bustu' for a gold dinar (this would be about 40,000 for a rupee). Sometimes the rate falls, and 12 'bustu' are exchanged for a gold dinar. The islanders barter them to the people of Bengal for rice, for they also form the currency in use in that country . . . These cowries serve also for barter with the negroes in their own land. I have seen them sold at Mali and Gugu (on the Niger) at the rate of 1,150 for a gold dinar."

Correa, a Portuguese, writing about A.D. 1561, states that:—

"'Gundras', or palm-wood boats from the Maldives come loaded with coir and 'caury' which are certain little white shells found among the islands in such abundance that whole vessels are laden with them, and which make a great trade in Bengala, where they are current as money."

CHAPTER VI

MALDIVIAN ARTS AND CRAFTS

AMONG the arts and crafts of the Maldives, lace-making is of importance. It is all hand-made pillow lace. Here, too, as in Ceylon, lace-making is practically all done by women, as their fine and delicate fingers are better suited to this work than those of men. The lace is often made with gold and silver thread imported from India and is used to ornament the upper portion of the dress worn by Maldivian women.

Besides the usual artisans, such as carpenters, masons, gold- and silver-smiths, copper-smiths and blacksmiths, there are stone-workers, cloth-weavers, net makers and sail weavers; of this last nearly all are women.

Maldivian lacquer work and finely woven mats are justly famed for their excellence and artistic beauty. Bell, writing of the Maldivian lacquer work, describes it thus:—

"In painting fancy articles such as favourite boats, lances, wooden dishes, axe handles, etc., the Maldivians have reached a degree of perfection, both in brilliancy and gradation of colour and beauty of design which it would be difficult to surpass . . . . . The best specimens are procurable at Tuladu in Malosmadulu Atoll.

"The delightful lacquer work industry of the Maldive Islands is said to be steadily declining. None is now executed apparently except for royalty and the nobles. The gradual disappearance of this unique art seems inevitable unless it can be specially fostered by local aid and foreign encouragement.

"Anxious to see the actual *modus operandi,* Ahmad Didi sent the only available worker at Male to my residence with a half-completed lacquered vase of wood, already lathe-turned and coloured a rich black with bright red borders.

"Simply standing before me holding the vase in his left hand the artificer with marvellous deftness ran first one, then the other of a couple of sharp-edged tools, not unlike short fine chisels, round the face of the black portions, gradually evolving therefrom exquisite foliaged tracery by cutting down to the pale yellow base coating of lacquer which underlies the black.

"The man worked rapidly and with no pattern as guide or other adventitious aid, the arabesque design assuming intricate shapes with machine-like accuracy.

"In 1921 there were, alas, only seventeen lacquer workers altogether in the Archipelago."

On my return to Ceylon I urged on the Maldivian Representative the necessity of en-

(Upper) GROUP OF BORAH MERCHANTS, MALÉ.

(Middle) LACE MAKING, MALDIVE ISLANDS.

(Lower) GATEWAY TO RESIDENTIAL QUARTERS, MALÉ.

deavouring to preserve and resuscitate this unique but dying industry. I pointed out that I felt sure that a ready market for the sale of this lacquer work could be found in Colombo among the numerous visitors and tourists who come to Ceylon who would, if they saw it, be willing to pay remunerative prices for it.

He was, however, not very sanguine about it, stating that the few workers who were left were not only slow, but capricious and unreliable and could not be depended on to complete an order within a given time. It seems a great pity however that such a beautiful art is now in danger of extinction.

I may state, however, that I gave one of the specimens I brought away with me to a young Sinhalese who had studied lacquer work in India and asked him whether he could make an exact replica of it. To my surprise and delight the copy he made was so well done that it differed in nowise from the original. This young man is at present employed in one of the Government carpentry schools in Ceylon and I have seen some beautiful specimens of lacquer work he has made. The lac used for colouring is not produced in the Maldives, but the crude shellac is imported from India and refined by methods known only to the few persons engaged in this work.

The weaving of mats is chiefly done by women.

Huwadu or Suvadiva Atoll, one of the most southern of the group and almost on the equator, is the centre of this industry as the rush from which the mats are made from is found there in abundance. Huwadu Atoll is three or four days sailing distance from Male, according to wind and weather. The colours used are black, yellowish-brown and white.

The mats range in size from an ordinary prayer mat, the size of a Persian prayer rug, to quite large ones, suitable for sleeping on or placing on a divan or on the floor. When spread on a bed they are delightfully cool and comfortable to sleep on during hot weather.

The mats are beautifully made and finely woven and the blending of colours is most artistic and very pleasing. The designs undoubtedly show the Persian and Arab influence and in this respect resemble some of those seen on Persian and Arab rugs. They are not dear and one can buy an excellent mat of beautiful design and workmanship for a comparatively small price.

One of the queer professions in the Maldives is that of charmers or magicians. There are also some astronomers who are necromancers as well, and all these are duly registered as such for census purposes.

The Maldivians for centuries past have earned among eastern peoples a reputation for their intimate knowledge of magic, sorcery, spells and charms. I remember just before leaving Ceylon on the voyage to Male my Malay chauffeur, a Moslem, imploring me to be very careful as the Maldivians were known for their arts in spell binding.

The ranks of the people were much depleted owing to an outbreak of influenza which occurred shortly after the war. The percentage of mortality was high and this was partly due to the fact that during the war years, when rice and food-stuffs were dear and difficult to procure, the natural powers of resistance to disease were weakened and although as previously stated a certain amount of dry grain such as millet and maize as well as yams are cultivated in many of the atolls, the quantity was quite insufficient for the needs of the inhabitants.

In consequence many of the people were reduced to living on roots and leaves of trees from sheer starvation. The lack of adequate supplies of rice was in fact so acute at the time, that I was told by Ahmad Didi that two islands in the group had been completely depopulated.

Bad as was the plight of the unfortunate islanders it might have been much worse were it not for the patrol of the British Navy, and their position would have been desperate indeed had it been found impossible to import any rice at all from India and Burma.

The Maldivian Government Representative stated in a brief note submitted to the Superintendent of Census, Ceylon, that there is now no naval force in the Maldives.

The seamen employed in the State vessels are called *kalasin,* or sailors. These men work in the brig and three schooners, and one or two buggalows owned by the State. Formerly, the *kalasin* were under the orders of a Vice-Admiral called *Ranahamadi,* and under him was a *Kuda Dandehelu* or Captain, who had command of the three most important vessels of the fourteen State vessels. A *dandehelu* or lieutenant was posted to each of the other eleven ships.

The *kalasin* are at liberty to look after their own affairs when not employed on the State vessels or engaged in other Government duties such as landing rice from ships, and the distribution of rice to the land forces, etc. The land forces consist of lascoreen or militia, the palace guards, and the gunners.

The lascoreen consists usually of six companies, each a hundred strong, and are used for police and ceremonial purposes.

The palace guards, numbering about twenty-five, are generally engaged in guarding the Sultan's residence. They are the only units who carry firearms during the day. The night guards, usually about fifty, are drawn from the lascoreens. The gunners are grouped into four batteries of twelve each, and are detailed to look after the various pieces of ordnance and to fire salutes when occasion arises.

There are several ranks or castes among the Maldivians. The Sultan and his family rank the highest of all. Intermarriage among the higher grades often occurs. A Didi is counted among one of the highest of these grades and can intermarry with the family of the Sultan.

Bell states that a Didi marrying a Manike lady raises her to his own rank—the Manikus being a grade immediately below a Didi, but the children of a Maniku father and Didi mother are actually not entitled to the appellation Didi, though this may be modified at times.

Pyrard states that in the case of a noble woman marrying a plebeian she retained her rank and upon her account the children were reckoned noble, but a woman of the lowest grade could not ennoble herself by marrying a nobleman.

Unlike Ceylon and some parts of India, the bridegroom receives no dowry with his wife, and is even obliged to meet the marriage expenses and also to maintain her and, if a man of substance, to settle a jointure upon her.

This procedure is correct and in accordance with orthodox Islamic tenets for it is the husband who must dower the wife.

On the Indian frontier more often than not the bridegroom buys his wife from the father, the price varying in accordance with the status of the man or the beauty of the girl.

The Muslims of Ceylon as well as some in India have succumbed to the Buddhist and Hindu custom of demanding a dowry from the parents of the girl, but there is no sanction for this in the *shariat,* or the revealed law of God according to the Musulman religion.

As regards the marriageable age, Pyrard states:—

"The males may marry when they will, but a female orphan cannot marry till she is fifteen. Indeed, if her father be alive, for the mother has no power, he marries her at ten or eleven and that to the first suitor whether old or young, provided his quality is in some measure suitable to hers, for they reckon it a great sin to keep the daughters unmarried."

The idea of it being a wrong thing to keep daughters unmarried is one that not only obtains in the Maldives but in most eastern countries, more especially among the Hindus.

A Hindu father considers himself utterly disgraced and liable to become an outcast if he has a daughter of marriageable age living in his house unwed.

In mediæval France the same idea was prevalent and hence the saying that "every saucepan must have its cover"

One morning I received an invitation from the

Indian merchants to accompany them out to the roadstead that evening and visit one of their new buggalows which had only arrived a few days previously on her maiden voyage.

Arrived at the harbour we boarded a trim sailing boat, a recent purchase. We ensconced ourselves comfortably in the stern sheets where numerous cushions and rugs had been placed and, having hoisted sail, we were soon speeding out of the inner harbour.

The sea was a bit choppy with a fresh wind blowing, but the boat behaved admirably. We finally arrived alongside the buggalow which had been dressed with flags.

On the poop a Persian carpet had been spread. The cushions and rugs were brought up from the boat and after we were made comfortable, tea and cigarettes were served.

One of the crew, a tall, well-built, but elderly man with snow-white hair and deep sunk eyes was detailed to assist in our entertainment. He was a typical old mariner, a native of Kutch, and except for his colour his rugged weather-beaten face would have made an admirable study of an East Coast fisherman. Most of his life he had spent at sea, he told us, but, apparently he was best acquainted with the east coast of Africa, having visited Zanzibar, Mombasa, and Dar-es-Salaam.

One of his turns was an exhibition of a Zanzibar nautch. His best rendering, however, I thought was the " Song of the Potter ". This was done squatted on the deck with a long pole in his hand, similar to that used by potters all over the east, to give an impetus to the wheel. As a character study it was perfect. He sang to the accompaniment of a large *dhol* or drum. At the end of each verse a chorus followed which the crew joined in lustily.

Other turns followed, one of the younger members of the crew, quite a boy, gave a very tolerable imitation of an Indian nautch girl including the usual *danse du ventre*.

After due compliments were made to the *Naukhoda* of the buggalow, we clambered down into the boat.

The moon was just rising, and the stars twinkled merrily in a sky of darkest blue above us. We had a fine sail back and as we entered the harbour the full moon rose out of a bank of cloud and turned the water to sparkling silver.

CHAPTER VII

THE CONVERSION TO ISLAM

THE conversion of the Maldivians to Islam dates from A.D. 1153. How this came about was explained to me by Ahmad Didi.

There are no existing records reaching very far back, but tradition has it that actual conversion took place about eight hundred years ago in this wise.

At that time the inhabitants were practically all either Buddhists or idolaters. Now, every month, a genie or demon would rise from the sea and demand a young virgin whom he would kill and devour.

One day there came to Male a very saintly man, well versed in the Koran, called Abul Barkat ul Barbari el Moghrebi, apparently from his name an Arab from Morocco. He lodged with a poor widow and her young daughter. The monthly sacrifice of a young girl was always decided by casting lots.

There came a day when El Moghrebi noticed that the widow was in great distress and could do nothing but weep and lament. On his asking the cause of her grief she told him that the lot had fallen to her daughter who was next day destined to be the sacrifice for that month. Hearing this he determined to frustrate the demon and informed the woman of his intention, saying that should he fail he would have at least saved her daughter, but that should he come safely through the ordeal it would be to the praise and glory of Allah the one God.

On the following day, being a beardless man, he dressed himself as a woman and was taken to the temple or idol house by the sea built for the purpose.

El Moghrebi entered alone and sitting down began to recite verses from the Koran. This he continued to do the whole night. Later the genie came with eyes of flame, but no sooner did he hear the Koran than he retreated and plunged into the sea. El Moghrebi remained till morning reciting the Koran and when the people came to the shore they found him alive and well, no harm whatsoever having befallen him.

He was brought before the king, who, astonished at what had happened, asked him how he had been able to escape from the monster.

"Oh King", replied El Moghrebi, "my faith is in Allah who has revealed himself in the Koran and through his holy prophet Mohammed. Know then there is but one god and He is Allah. Through His mercy and compassion I have been saved from the clutches of the demon. Cease, therefore, to worship idols and turn to the true Faith, both you and your people, and thereafter will there be no cause for fear of the demon."

El Moghrebi then expounded the doctrine of Islam to the King and his people. The King was so impressed that he begged El Moghrebi to stay yet another month, and if he were then again able to escape from the genie he agreed to accept Islam.

When the second month came the King with his nobles and many others accompanied El Moghrebi to the temple by the shore and left him to pass the night alone there. On the following morning when they returned they found him sitting as before reciting verses from the Koran.

The King then ordered the temple to be destroyed and the images it contained to be broken in pieces and he and his people were all converted to Islam.

Ibn Batuta states that the sect into which they entered was that of the Mogrebin of Ibn Malik who is greatly revered. The Maldivians are all Sunnis as opposed to the Shiahs, much the same difference as between Protestants and Catholics among Christians.

The first part of the story in some respects bears a resemblance to the legend of Saint George and the Dragon.

Two hundred years after this the Maldive Islands were visited by Ibn Batuta who, impelled by religious enthusiasm, set out from his native city of Tangiers in A.D. 1324 and devoted twenty-eight years to a pilgrimage of which he has left a record which, says Sir Emerson Tennent, "has entitled him to rank amongst the most remarkable travellers of any age or country".

On his journey to Serendib, or Ceylon, where he intended making a pilgrimage to Adam's Peak, he visited the Maldive Islands where he spent some very considerable time. Whilst there, filled with religious zeal, he also expounded the Koranic doctrine to the Sultan and his people. He was held in high esteem and afterwards the office of Qazi or Judge was conferred on him.

He married three wives, but when his relations through them became numerous and powerful the fear and jealousy of the Vizier was stirred against him, the latter seeing in him a possible and powerful rival. The Vizier plotted and worked against him.

Realizing the state of affairs Ibn Batuta determined to leave Male, and he "then divorced all my wives except one who had a young child and left that island for those which stretch out before it".

Ibn Batuta's account of the Maldivian conversion is practically the same as that related to me except that in his description of the genie or demon he states that its appearance was that of a ship filled with candles. He avers, too, in his

1.

2.

3.

4.

1. THE SULTAN'S LANCERS
2. ENTRANCE TO MALÉ HARBOUR
3. SHRINE OF YUSUF SHAMSHUDDIN EL TABRIZI
4. HUKURU MISKIT, MALÉ.

narrative that he himself once actually saw the genie and " it resembled a ship filled with candles and torches ".

Ibn Batuta is said to have been followed later by Yusuf Shamsuddin Tabrizi who, as his name implies, came from Tabriz in Persia. He was a very pious and holy man and to this day his name is held in the greatest veneration by all the islanders. The Medu Ziarat, one of the finest shrines in Male, was erected in the middle of the twelfth century to his saintly memory which I do not think will ever die in the hearts of the Maldivians. It stands opposite to the Hukuru Miskit, the chief Mosque in Male.

From what I could gather, however, there seems to be some considerable amount of doubt as to whether Tabrizi was not after all really the original El Moghrebi, and the date of his actual arrival confused owing to the loss of records and the mists of antiquity.

Harking back to the narrative of Ibn Batuta, it is more than probable that the actual reason for his hurried departure from Male was that having had honours and favours conferred on him he began with typical Arab arrogance to " throw his weight about ". Possibly he may have bullied and browbeaten those with whom he came in contact and especially those over whom he had authority, to the verge of desperation.

Finding, perhaps, he had gone too far and that the place was becoming too hot to hold him he may have decided that discretion was the better part of valour and shaken the sand of Male from his feet.

It is also conceivable that the story of the conversion of the islanders to Islam by Abul Barkat ul Barbari el Moghrebi originated with him. Being a Moroccan himself he would naturally desire that the credit of such conversion should be given to one of his own countrymen, for, undoubtedly, the title el Moghrebi denotes a Moroccan. It is quite possible, therefore, that Yusuf Shamsuddin Tabrizi was actually the man through whose efforts the Maldivians were converted and not Abul Barkat ul Barbari at all, and the statement that he followed after Ibn Batuta is incorrect.

On the occasion of one of my later visits to the Indian merchants I heard of a very interesting young man, a close relation of the Didis, and second cousin to the present Sultan, who was then living in Male in more or less obscurity.

I determined to visit him and called on him at his little office which also served him as a study. Husain Hilmy Didi received me with every courtesy and kindness and afterwards we had many long talks together. He had been a student in an Indian University and had returned to Male after completing his education.

I found him to be a very well-informed and well-read man, and keen with regard to the progress and development of his mother land. He was anxious, too, to ameliorate the general conditions of the people. He chafed at the age-old conservatism and absolutism of the Maldivian Government and the general apathy towards any modern thought and the antagonism displayed at any suggestion of reforms or for a more popular form of Government. But, alas ! the way of all reformers, like that of transgressors, is hard, and only men with a firm resolve and undaunted spirit can ever hope to win through. Some have blazed the trail and left others to complete their work; others more fortunate have lived to see their desires come to fruition. Hilmy, I am glad to say, has since I first met him become one of the latter, and although it has taken some years of patient waiting, I think great things can be expected of him.

I found he had a well-stocked book-case of interesting and instructive works by well-known writers. He was also very interested in photography and showed me some very fine photographs he had taken. His knowledge, however, was not only gained from books but from personal experience.

Now, the Maldives are peculiar in this respect, that it is not a very difficult matter to get there and for a casual visitor or representative of another Government departure thence offers no difficulties whatever. For Maldivian nationals, however, it is not so easy.

Even Pyrard, after being ship-wrecked at a time when little was known of European countries, found himself virtually a prisoner and unable to leave the islands. His movements were so closely watched that he could find no way of escape and he was compelled to stay there for five years at the pleasure of the Sultan and much against his own will.

The reason he gives is because " few Europeans ever so much as touch there and none go to reside unless they are unfortunately cast away as I was and even in that case it is most likely they never get away.

" Nor had I and my companions ever escaped but by the greatest accident in the world which was the sudden arrival of a fleet from Bengale with some forces. The king of the islands at the sight of those vessels fled and I having contrived to stay behind with my comrades we went aboard those vessels and made our escape from captivity."

He eventually succeeded in reaching Bengal safely after a voyage which lasted for over a month.

When Hilmy returned to Male after completing his education in India it is possible that imbued with the zeal of youth and the desire to introduce reforms he may have expressed his ideas more freely than was discreet. In consequence he was viewed with suspicion, if not resentment, by those in authority, including some of his own relatives in high places, who clinging to the old order of things had no desire to lose their privileges and prerogatives which had been handed down to them for centuries.

The result was that things were made not too comfortable for him, and when he finally made up his mind to leave the Maldives and return to India or elsewhere he found himself virtually a prisoner. His movements were so carefully watched that it was impossible for him to leave Male.

On the occasions when I visited him I had to do so with the greatest circumspection. Not that I made any secret of doing so, for I did not wish to be involved in any way or give any cause for suspicion to a Government whose guest I was. I was careful always to mention in conversation to Ahmad Didi whenever I had seen Hilmy. The fact was, we were mutually drawn to one another and naturally he was glad to meet someone from the outside world to talk to and for the common exchange ot views and ideas.

On the day before I sailed to return to Ceylon he gave me a book from his small library inscribed "as a token of your visit to my humble study" which I have with me still.

He also presented me with a magnificent "Triton" shell as a souvenir of my visit. It is one of the largest of its kind I have ever seen and measures no less than fifteen inches in length with a circumference of nearly nineteen inches at its broadest part and is most beautifully coloured.

It had rained on one or two days during my stay in Male, and this tended to make the weather very hot and sultry and at times not unlike a vapour bath, more especially when there was an absence of wind.

Although the climate and temperature are not unlike those experienced in many parts of the low country in Ceylon, the fact of the islands being so little above sea-level might prove more enervating for any one unaccustomed to these conditions who resided for any length of time there.

Two days prior to my departure Ahmad Didi informed me that his brother Abdul Majid Didi, Bodu Baderi Manikufanu, to give him his full Maldivian title, Prime Minister and Chief Treasurer to His Highness the Sultan, was now recovered from his fever and would give himself the pleasure of calling to see me that afternoon.

Accompanied by Ahmad Didi and several retainers he arrived about five o'clock. He was a sturdy man of medium height, of about forty-five, with a strong face and good features.

Ahmad Didi had previously informed me that his brother was not very strong in English so we all conversed in Hindustani.

Abdul Majid Didi appeared to have travelled a good deal, especially in India where he had visited many of the chief cities, such as Calcutta, Lucknow, Agra and Delhi. He has also been to Srinagar in Kashmir. This gave us a common ground for conversation and I found his Hindustani was excellent.

Although he is Ahmad Didi's younger brother, or rather half-brother, by another mother, he was, I believe, the real "power behind the throne". His word was apparently law, and he practically directed everything.

I realized therefore, I was in the presence of one who might with justice have been called the Maldivian Mussolini. From what I had heard about him I gathered that if he were not acquainted with "The Prince" he had, nevertheless, adopted a policy similar to that which Machiavelli advocates for rulers in his book.

"One ought to be both feared and loved, but it is much safer to be feared than to be loved if one of the two has to be wanting."

Coffee was then served and shortly afterwards I was presented with a *hadiya,* in remembrance of my visit. This consisted of a large roll of the finest Maldivian mats of varied and beautiful design, some charming samples of the best

Maldivian lacquer work, which money cannot buy here as it is only made for the Sultan and his entourage, and a box containing, I should think, every variety of shell found in these islands. The colouring of many of the shells was very beautiful and varied and the shape of several of them most extraordinary.

After receiving my thanks and conversing a little further Abdul Majid Didi bade me good-bye.

The following day Ahmad Didi called and brought with him presents from the Sultan. There were three specimens of ambergris, white, brown and black, some more pieces of delightful lacquer work, and a roll of fine Maldivian mats. These were, I was told, a parting gift to me from His Highness.

That evening I was royally entertained to dinner by my friends the Indian merchants. The dishes were as varied as they were numerous—several kinds of curry made of chicken, prawns, and vegetables, and a perfectly gorgeous *pilau* of rice, in which almonds, raisins, and pistachio nuts had been included.

There were also various kinds of sweetmeats, such as *halwa,* and Maldivian honey sweets made from the juice of the coconut-palm. The dessert consisted of mangoes of fine taste and flavour, bananas and dried apricots and raisins. Altogether a most kingly repast.

There was a wonderful sunrise the following

morning which was the day of my departure. It was the tenth of May, and I had spent a very pleasant fortnight in Male.

Clouds began to gather later on and the sky became overcast.

Ahmad Didi accompanied me in the State boat to the buggalow and there bade me good-bye. He had been most kind to me and I shall always feel most grateful to him for all he did for me to make my stay in Male as pleasant and interesting as possible.

Shortly after the departure of Ahmad Didi several of the Indian merchants arrived in their sailing boat. They were all most kind and brought with them several kinds of fruit and other good things for my use on the voyage.

The clouds which had been gathering for some time now burst. There was a very heavy thunderstorm, followed by torrential rain. Fortunately, however, it soon cleared again.

My Indian friends took their departure after many protestations of friendship and good wishes for the voyage. Their hospitality and kindness to me during my sojourn I shall always look back upon as a very pleasant memory.

CHAPTER VIII

THE RETURN VOYAGE

ALTHOUGH I had left the jetty at Male a little after nine o'clock in the morning and reached the "Nurani" shortly after, by the time both anchors were weighed, the ship's boat hoisted aboard, and sail set, it was nearly three o'clock in the afternoon.

The crews of buggalows have a curious chanty when heaving up the anchor or pulling on sail ropes. Two men usually constitute themselves as leaders and the repeated refrain is "jumsa" which is something equivalent to our "heave oh".

They sing a verse of two lines—any jingle that rhymes which they make up out of their heads at the time—and then shout "jumsa"; the others join in with "jumsa" in chorus. Sometimes the rhyme is anything but fit for ears polite, but what matters it so the work is done.

At last we began to make way, slowly at first, and then as the wind freshened from the south-west the ship increased her speed.

I had now spent a fortnight full of novelty and interest at Male.

Soon the town receded in the distance and we rounded the eastern end of the island. The atolls with their green islands melted from our view. Overhead was a grey, watery sky with the promise of more rain. Rain fell during most of the night. About one o'clock next morning a strong wind was blowing which necessitated shortening sail.

Towards dawn the wind fell, and before mid-day the sails were flapping idly and we were more or less becalmed. Fortunately, the sky was overcast as otherwise it would have been stiflingly hot.

Early in the afternoon there was a slight breeze and with it came a drizzling, drenching rain. Everything on the poop-deck became wet and clammy. Still better that than to seek refuge below deck, for our cargo of Maldive fish which was stowed in the holds running under the main deck had a most pungent and penetrating odour. It also sets up a certain amount of heat which come up right through the seams of the deck. If one can imagine what a stable or byre which had not been cleaned out for some time smells like, and add to this "an ancient and fish-like smell", it will give some faint idea of its pungency and strength. I found the only thing to do was to smoke incessantly.

Another drawback was that outward bound with rice and general cargo the ship seemed fairly free of such vermin as ants and cockroaches, but now with a cargo of fish and copra aboard these seemed to swarm. There was, besides, the ordinary reddish-brown cockroach, another dirty-grey coloured one which seemed far more in evidence than the other. Copra beetles, too, began to make their appearance; also a peculiar kind of black maggot, engendered from the fish which, having crawled through the deck seams, were to be met with everywhere. Even lying on deck one felt occasionally one or more of these filthy creatures crawling over one, which was a most unpleasant sensation. I thanked heaven, however, that there were no bugs in evidence. I heard afterwards that wherever there are large numbers of cockroaches bugs are seldom found.

I determined, however, to take things philosophically and not be over-sensitive or too critical.

During the day there were some flies as well, but luckily not very large in number.

The weather cleared a little towards evening.

About seven o'clock a large tunny fish was caught on the line trailing in the wake of the ship. It struggled desperately but at length after a great deal of trouble it was successfully gaffed with a boat hook and hauled on board.

It seemed to have tremendous strength in its tail which it lashed savagely when lying on the deck. The crew of course were delighted as it meant a feast for them. They proceeded to cut it up and after keeping aside what they required for the time being proceeded to pickle the remainder in brine. The flesh was of a dark red colour not unlike butcher meat. Unfortunately there were no scales on board with which to weigh it, but I measured it and found it to be 3½ feet in length with a girth of 27 inches and 26 inches from the tip of one fin to the tip of the other, and the length of each fin was 11 inches.

Near midnight the clouds had disappeared and there was a fine starry expanse of sky and a favourable wind blowing. Unfortunately, this did not last very long and by four o'clock it began to rain again very heavily.

The morning dawned a dull grey with a fairly heavy sea running and the wind blowing strong from the south-west. Jamaldin, my Malay servant, along with two other Ceylonese Moormen belonging to Galle who were returning to Ceylon were all horribly sea-sick. Poor devils, I was sorry for them.

There are quite a number of Ceylon Moormen or Moslems in Male. They are as a rule petty traders and shop-keepers and usually stay in Male for two or three years at a time and then return for six months to their families in Ceylon.

The Borah merchants' representatives do much the same only they go to their homes in India.

The weather cleared in the afternoon and we had brilliant sunshine. This enabled the crew as well as myself to dry some of our clothes and bedding which were more or less sodden with the previous night's rain.

Towards evening some of the crew with rod and line managed to kill half a dozen small tunny fish averaging I should say about four to five pounds each in weight.

The stars came out at night but there was very little wind and our progress slow in consequence. About midnight the stars were suddenly blotted out and then flashes of lightning lit up thick black clouds in the background.

We experienced a heavy storm of wind with a rising sea which compelled us to shorten sail.

After the wind had abated somewhat it began to rain again but ceased about five o'clock. The morning was grey and cloudy and the sky overcast with the sun feebly attempting to struggle through.

About seven o'clock another large fish, also a tunny, was caught on the log line and again the boat-hook came in useful for gaffing. This fish was even bigger than the one killed two days previously. Its length was 4½ feet, girth 32 inches, the length of each fin was 13 inches and the length from tip to tip of each fin 36 inches. It was more like a small barrel and must have been of considerable weight.

I ate some of it later. It had very few bones and was sweet and flaky but a little coarse.

The ship's cook boiled some excellently well for me and also made some more of it into a most palatable curry.

The clouds lifted and we had a fine sunny afternoon though rather warm. It became cloudy again in the evening and the wind began to rise. Heavy rain fell about seven o'clock and the strength of the wind increased. It continued to rain off and on during the night but the wind held and we made excellent speed.

The morning of the 14th May was grey with gathering storm clouds. The horizon gradually took on an inky hue. The general outlook reminded me of nothing so much as a stormy day in the Bay of Biscay or the North Sea.

It was now the fifth day since I had left Male.

Shortly after seven o'clock that morning we experienced another very heavy rain storm accompanied by a strong wind. The seas were running very high but the buggalow behaved well and sailed like a duck, shipping hardly any water.

A school of dolphins passed us swimming swiftly and gracefully through the waves. In spite of the heavy weather the ship kept up a good speed.

About nine o'clock we sighted a steamer making eastwards. It was the first one I had seen for some weeks. By this time we were well in the track of steamers going both eastward and westward. The sun struggled through the clouds a little after ten o'clock which allowed for observations to be taken. After this the wind increased to a gale and the seas became mountainous in height.

By noon it was found necessary to lower the main sail and hoist a jib. This took some little time as these sails are rather clumsy to handle, especially in heavy weather. Whilst this was being done we lay in the trough of the sea and rolled and pitched to a tremendous extent. Although it stopped raining for a little shortly after noon the gale had in no way abated.

As the day wore on the storm increased in strength and intensity. From the observations taken that morning the *Naukhoda* reckoned we were some eighty odd miles off Colombo.

All sail having had eventually to be furled, we were now scudding under bare poles before the wind. It was practically impossible to stand on the deck and even when I lay down I had to have two bamboos lashed on either side of me to keep me from sliding about.

The night settled down very wet and the storm still raged. The wind fairly roared through the rigging. The slip of awning I had over me leaked like a sieve, being only sacking, but luckily I had provided myself before leaving with a rubber ground-sheet which came in very useful. It was altogether a most horribly uncomfortable night, and it was with difficulty I was able to snatch even a few minutes sleep at a time. About midnight we sighted the lights of a steamer which had evidently left Colombo.

About 4 a.m. on the 15th May, amidst lightning, thunder and rain, and with a howling gale blowing, we were just able to make out the flash of the Colombo light. I never before felt that light so welcome. It was old Jiwa, the *Naukhoda*, who had spent an anxious night of it, who first pointed it out to me in the mirk. "See, Sahib, the Colombo light. It is a good light, and we thank God for it has saved many of our lives", he said.

Dawn found us wallowing in a heavy beam sea. About seven o'clock a smaller size of mainsail was with great difficulty hoisted, but once this was up our speed increased and the ship steadied up considerably. Soon the coast line of Ceylon began to loom up in a dark line. Then, gradually, coconut palms and buildings could be made out. We found we were nearly abreast of Mount Lavinia.

The rain continued to fall torrentially and the wind was very strong with high seas. Gradually the Colombo breakwater came into view. With great difficulty we entered the harbour and then ran into smooth water. By half-past ten that morning we dropped anchor safely. It was not long before I was ashore, where in spite of stormy conditions several of my friends awaited me at the jetty and gave me a warm welcome, and their congratulations on my safe return.

I must say that after my arrival I felt very fit and looked very bronzed. The experience I had had was to me in every way a most interesting one. Many a time since as I have watched the white sails of a buggalow making her way out of Colombo harbour on her voyage to Male an intense longing has come over me to repeat the voyage. And, perhaps, some day I shall do so again. *Quien Sabe* !

Ten days after my return I suddenly succumbed to the Maldivian malaria and it was fully three weeks before I had got over the worst of it.

As regards the gallant buggalow "Nurani", alas ! I regret to add she no more sails the seas.

In May, 1930, just four years after my return, the "Nurani" on her last voyage with a cargo of Maldive fish and copra and four passengers had encountered a heavy storm after three days sail from Male and sprung a leak. Her sails were torn to ribbons, and the snapping of the main mast was the final blow. After terrible hardships the men one night sighted the Beruwela lighthouse on the south-west coast of Ceylon and allowing the vessel to drift towards the lighthouse, anchor was cast the following morning. The storm, however, which had abated somewhat, again gathered strength, with the result that the anchor cable parted and the rudder broke. Water gained on the pumps rapidly. The crew and passengers then took to the boat and were able to row to land. When nearing the shore, however, the boat capsized.

The people of Katukurunda came to their assistance, and helped the stranded men ashore, and fed and housed them. The "Nurani" herself became a total wreck.

I met old Jiwa, the *Naukhoda,* shortly afterwards and he related to me the terrible experience he had been through.

I am glad to say he is still alive and well, but having become too old now to command a buggalow he is retained as a pensioner by my Borah friend whose loss by the foundering of his ship was a very heavy one as neither the vessel nor the merchandise were covered by insurance.

CHAPTER IX

THE NEW MALDIVIAN CONSTITUTION

"THE people's flag is coloured red", and so is that of the Maldivian Government—there is now another flag used as well with a red border round a square of emerald green on which a white star is imposed—and there the analogy with what is a very conservative form of government and the ideal of Socialists and Communists begins and ends.

As recently as 1932, on the 22nd December in that year, the Sultan Muhammad Shams-ud-Din Iskandar III. granted a Constitution to the people on more or less democratic lines and proclaimed this fact at a Durbar held on that date.

Elaborate arrangements were made for the inauguration of the new system and headmen and others had been invited from all the outlying islands to be present at the function and suitable accommodation had been provided for them.

The Sultan in his address at the Durbar stated that "The Maldives is a kingdom which has been paying tribute to the great British Government and has enjoyed its protection against foreign enemies". Nevertheless, it is a completely independent State.

The Constitution was ushered in with great pomp and ceremony. In granting the Constitution the Sultan had intimated that he was renouncing his royal prerogatives which had been held by him and his predecessors for a period of over eight hundred years.

The wave of democracy which has made itself felt not only in many European countries after the war but also in the Orient, finally broke on the shores of the Maldives. Some of the younger generation who had either studied or travelled abroad were imbued with the idea of effecting a change in the old order of things. As several of them were related either by blood or marriage to government officials of high standing belonging to the Maldivian aristocracy, and even to the family of the Sultan himself, I should imagine it was not a very difficult matter for them to persuade the Sultan to agree to a change in the régime.

In order to proclaim to his subjects and to the world at large how progressive the Maldives were and how eager to follow in the wake of universal democracy the Sultan intimated that the new Constitution had been granted to the people at his own expressed desire.

There is no doubt, of course, that the Moslem religion is one of the most democratic in the world. The Sultan on his throne and the beggar in the street being co-religionists are brothers, if not in actual fact, at any rate in theory.

Let us, however, for a moment examine the details of the new Constitution as set forth.

It consists of a People's Assembly, of forty-seven elected members. These forty-seven members are elected as follows.

Large atolls to elect four members for each, two members for each of the smaller atolls, one member for Mulaku Island, and four members elected by the four wards of Male.

The necessary qualifications for voters are they must be Maldivian subjects and of the male sex. The Maldivians, unlike Ceylon, have not as yet yielded to the importunities of the members of the fair sex and granted them suffrage.

The voter must not be less than twenty-five years of age. He must be able to read and write Arabic and Maldivian characters and be a resident of the place for twelve months prior to the date of commencement of the registration of the voter's list.

Members of the People's Assembly shall be elected once a year.

The Legislative Council consists of twenty-eight members of whom seven members shall be nominated by the Sultan. Four members shall be elected by the voters of four wards in Male and seventeen members shall be elected by the People's Assembly. The election takes place at Male. The Legislative Council will continue for a period of five years, fresh elections taking place every five years. The President of the Legislative Council shall be the Prime Minister, the Vice-President to be elected by the Council.

Some of the necessary qualifications for members are that they must be Muslims and of the Sunni sect. They must be twenty-five years of age and free men, i.e., that they are not in debt or financially embarrassed. They must be Maldivians and persons of integrity who have not lost the confidence and respect of the public. They must be able to read and write Maldivian and Arabic characters and possess a good knowledge of arithmetic. They must not be persons found guilty of any offence against the State who have not been pardoned for that offence, and they should be acquainted with the affairs of their constituencies.

From the above it will be noted that there is no latitude with regard to religious toleration, for not only must a member be a Muslim but he must also belong to the Sunni sect of that religion.

This qualification of course also applies to the Sultan himself in the same manner that the occupant of the throne of Great Britain must be a Christian of the Protestant religion. As, however, all Maldivians are Moslems of the Sunni sect this does not incur any hardship.

The Council of Ministers are responsible for upholding the dignity and rights of the State and carrying out all the affairs of the Kingdom.

The Sultan appoints the Prime Minister in consultation with the Legislative Council, the selection being made from among its members.

Thereafter other Ministers are selected with the permission of the Sultan by the Prime Minister from among members of the Legislative Council. These Ministers are ex-officio members of the Legislative Council.

It is stipulated *inter alia* that Ministers must have the ability and knowledge of the working of the departments in their charge and to carry out the work efficiently.

All orders issued from the Council of Ministers must bear the signature of the Prime Minister as well as the signature of the Minister to whose department such orders relate.

The Council of Ministers will be held responsible for decrees issued under the Seal of the Sultan as such decrees are issued on the advice of the Ministers.

No Minister while holding office is permitted to buy any share of a trading concern or send out to islands goods for trade in his name or conduct business in a shop. The italics are mine.

This regulation could, I imagine, be circumvented by the employment of either an agent or proxy bearing another name.

If a vote of no confidence is passed by the Legislative Council in the People's Assembly on the Council of Ministers it is incumbent on the Ministers to report the fact to the Sultan and place their resignations in his hands.

The Sultan shall thereafter proceed to elect a new Council of Ministers, but until a new Council of Ministers is formed the old Council shall carry on the Government.

Thus, there are three Majlis or Councils. The Sultan will summon once every year a People's Assembly for the purpose of advising and criticizing the administration of the two other Majlis with the Majlis of Ministers and the Legislative Majlis.

To anyone unacquainted with the general mass of the inhabitants of these islands and their extreme ignorance with regard to any new form of Government the Constitution may appear quite a reasonable one.

It remains to be seen how this grafting of a democratic régime on to what was previously more or less an absolute monarchy is going to work in practice.

Although ostensibly democratic in outline it is not a difficult matter for those with power and influence so to arrange that the plums of office fell to them.

The total population of the Maldivian Archipelago, as I have stated previously, is between 70,000 and 80,000. The annual value of trade is about £500,000 and the revenue between £30,000 and £40,000. A considerable sum from the latter amount is reserved for the Sultan's Court and his Civil List. The salaries of the Ministers have, however, been fixed on a scale seemingly out of all proportion to the revenue of the country, and the relative importance of their positions as compared with those of many larger and more opulent States in Europe, and even the Imperial Japanese Government.

The Prime Minister is in receipt of a salary of Rs. 12,000, or very nearly £1,000 per annum, and each of the other six Ministers receives half this amount.

Living is by no means dear in the Maldives, even allowing that foodstuffs such as cereals and other articles of use have to be imported. The emoluments to Ministers would, therefore, appear to have been fixed on a very generous scale.

Abdul Hamid Didi retained his position as Maldivian Representative to the Government of Ceylon. Ahmad Didi, his elder brother, remained, as previously, Private Secretary to the Sultan.

As regards the Ministers themselves, the Sultan nominated as the head of the Government or Prime Minister Amir Muhammad Farid Didi, under whose guidance six Ministers were selected out of the twenty-eight members for the administration of the twelve departments provided in the Constitution.

The Cabinet of Ministers, therefore, was composed of the following:—

Amir Muhammad Farid Didi, the Prime Minister, the son of Amir Haji Abdul Majid Didi, Ranna Baderi Kilegefanü. Amir Hasan Farid Didi, brother of the Prime Minister, was appointed Minister of Finance and of Foreign Affairs.

When I visited Male in 1926, Abdul Majid Didi, the brother of Ahmad Didi and Abdul Hamid Didi, was Prime Minister and Treasurer under the old régime. He was undoubtedly a very strong and able man. He subsequently resigned his office and left Male, and was till very recently residing in Egypt.

The ages of his two sons at the time the Constitution was granted were respectively twenty-nine and twenty-seven—both young enough to hold such high office.

Mohamed Amin Didi, aged twenty-five, son of Ahmad Didi, and therefore a cousin of the Prime Minister, and son-in-law of Husain Didi Salahaudin, Minister of Justice, became Minister for Commerce.

Husain Didi Salahaudin, at one time Chief Justice of the High Court, was made Minister of Justice.

Ibrahim Ali Didi, son of the late Ali Didi, was given the Ministry of Health and Agriculture.

Ahmad Kamil Didi, half brother of Abdul Hamid Didi, the Maldivian Representative in Ceylon, and Abdul Majid Didi, and uncle of the Prime Minister, was appointed Minister of Home Affairs and of Education.

Muhammad Didi, son of the late Amir Ali Dhori Mena Kilegefanu, was made Minister of Public Works.

It will thus be seen that the Constitution while professing to be a democratic institution has made a close family preserve of the Ministry and high offices of the Government and one is inclined to wonder when and how the will of the people is to prevail.

It may be argued of course that the Ministry is composed of educated and experienced men and that it would be difficult to find others as suitable from among the great bulk of the people. This may be true in the case of the Maldivian Representative in Ceylon and of his brother Ahmad Didi, but it is doubtful whether this is equally applicable to the others.

Some of the Ministers, I understand, from a letter which appeared recently in the Ceylon Press, are themselves also engaged in trade and enjoy certain privileges such as a special three months' credit when they buy goods from the Government, which have been collected in the way of duty. They are further entitled to certain discounts which are denied to the ordinary trader. In this, their position appears to be unique, as it is hardly to be conceived that any other well constituted government would allow of their own Ministers trading with it.

If there be any truth in this statement it constitutes a violation of one of the regulations laid down for the observance of Ministers.

To quote the same authority, "the general condition of the masses remains the same, and we have the spectacle in miniature of a limited monarchy with the actual Government in the hands of an oligarchy who are all members of an exclusive and closely allied aristocracy. This would be harmless enough if the people could afford the luxury, but this they cannot do, nor is there any prospect of their being able to do so in the near future".

Towards the middle of 1933, in the first year of this Constitution, the relations between the Borah merchants and the Maldivian Government began to be strained. There were charges and counter-charges between the two parties. The Maldivian Government averred that the country had now come to the limit of exploitation by the Borahs which had been carried on for years, and that strong measures must be adopted to curb the rapacity and sharp practice which obtained in the dealings of these Indian merchants with the simple and unsophisticated islanders.

Accusations were made of unfair dealing, giving short weight in rice and charging a high price for it, whilst at the same time squeezing the people down to accept what was much less than the legitimate value for Maldive fish which was sold in Ceylon at a handsome profit. When the word "price" is mentioned, this does not mean money, as practically the whole trade in the Maldives is conducted by barter which obviates any complex questions of exchange and currency.

Pyrard mentions that in his time the Maldives were "well frequented with merchants".

There is no doubt of course that in the past the astute Borah merchants have amassed considerable wealth through their trade with the Maldives. This has been due to their energy and business acumen coupled with first-hand knowledge of market prices. That some of them have also resorted to malpractices in their dealings and have taken an unfair advantage of their position when dealing with a simple and primitive people there is, I think, little room for doubt, but it is equally unfair to level these charges against the whole community, many of the members of which are known and respected in Ceylon as being men of probity.

The Maldivian Government decided that it was

necessary to declare the importation of rice a Government monopoly as the only means of reducing the price of this cereal for the people, declaring at the same time that the sole aim of such a measure was to assist the Maldivians and not for the Government to profit by it.

Kamil Didi, the Minister for Home Affairs, was sent by the Sultan and his Government to Ceylon, as mentioned by him in a lengthy statement which was published in the Ceylon Press early in August, 1933, for the purpose of inaugurating a steamer service between Colombo and Male in collaboration with the Maldivian Representative in Ceylon. The main object of establishing a steamer service being to help the Maldivians in their desire to develop their home industries and to reduce the price of food-stuffs, particularly of rice. He expressed his gratitude and thanks to the Government of Ceylon for agreeing to assist the Maldivian Government towards the successful running of the proposed steamer service.

Shortly prior to the advent of the Maldivian Home Minister to Ceylon there had been a strike among the employees of the Borah merchants in Male, which lead to the deportation of some of them. The reason given by Kamil Didi for this strike, which also was the cause of some small disturbances, was that the malpractices previously mentioned, which were resorted to by the merchants prior to the Constitution, having been effectively stopped by the appointment of inspectors before whom fish, rice, and other food-stuffs had to be weighed and the merchants prosecuted if found to be tampering with weights, and, similarly, the Maldivians were dealt with if they were discovered bringing any foreign matter with the fish for sale.

It so happened that an employee of the merchants was fined for some offence and on the following day all the shops were closed. On being asked by the Government for the reason for this the merchants stated that it was because of the celebration of the birthday of one of their titular saints. The following day the shops still remained closed, and on further enquiry the merchants are stated to have said that they had also learned to fine people and they would fine their employees if they sold goods to the Maldivians. They further stated that their employees had drawn up a petition to be presented to the Government and if their terms were accepted they would open their shops. On the third day of the strike at the instance of the Minister of Commerce a meeting of the Cabinet was held. A conference was then held at the office of the Prime Minister at which the merchants reiterated what they had previously told the Minister of Commerce.

The Government at the same time were aware that the merchants had given orders to their buggalows not to unload goods or ship any goods from the islands. The merchants were advised to end the strike and to forward a petition setting forth their grievances to which the Government would give favourable consideration. At this the merchants demurred and replied that unless the Government were prepared to accept all the terms in their petition they would not call off the strike.

Whilst the Government were in this quandary it so happened that H.M.S. "Hawkins", the Flag Ship of the East Indies Squadron, with H. E. the Naval Commander-in-Chief Rear-Admiral Dunbar-Nasmith, V.C.,* on board, arrived. The same evening a Minister visited the Admiral and through him a wireless message was despatched to the Maldivian Representative in Ceylon requesting him to consult the Ceylon Government.

The following day, at the request of the Sultan, the Naval Commander-in-Chief invited the Borah merchants and some Ministers to a Conference on board ship. The Admiral was able to effect a settlement and asked the merchants to re-open their shops and to represent their grievances to the Maldivian Government, which on its side promised to redress any grievances which might exist. Apparently, however, no petition was subsequently presented by the merchants.

* Now Sir Martin Dunbar-Nasmith, V.C., K.C.B., R.N.

The above is more or less in accordance with the statement of Kamil Didi.

He also mentions that during the seven months the Constitution had been in existence the salaries of all Government Civil Servants had been increased, that trial by jury had been established, and that over thirty-five Bills of Legislative enactments had been promulgated.

In reply to the statement of the Maldivian Minister of Home Affairs a Borah merchant who is also Secretary of the Maldivian Merchants' Association submitted to the Ceylon Press the other side of the question.

Among other matters he stated that there were at present forty-six firms owning fifty-two business places in the Maldives, some of which had been in existence for over a century. The foreign trading community consisted of two hundred and fifty Borahs, fifty Moplahs from Malabar, and fifty Ceylon Moors.

This community had recently erected a mosque costing over fifty thousand rupees and they also were the owners of eighteen buggalows with which a regular trade is carried on between Ceylon and the Maldives. The amount vested in this business exceeds twenty-five lakhs of rupees (over £180,000), the principal imports of rice, sugar and piece goods into the Maldives being estimated at thirty lakhs of rupees—over £225,000. He acknowledges that ninety-five per cent. of the trade is in the hands of the Borah merchants but at the same time emphasizes that the business is not without considerable risk in that neither ships nor cargoes are underwritten, insurance companies not being prepared to accept the risk. Two buggalows were totally wrecked within the last two years which involved a loss of £15,000. He denies the allegation of false weights and measures and states that under the guise of Nationalism the present Maldivian Government is seeking to destroy a trade which has taken years to build up. A campaign of pin-prick persecution was started by the Maldivian police, who are a body of men untrained and uninstructed and in the absence of anything serious to do are constantly arresting and prosecuting the employees in the shops on the most frivolous charges. That these charges are tried by the Minister of Finance and no defence is possible. The employees in the shops, who are in receipt of small salaries, finding themselves fined out of all their wages struck work as a protest. In this they were neither aided nor abetted by their principals. On being given an assurance that their grievances would be remedied they returned to work after a three-days' strike.

He avers that the Minister exaggerated this incident as a trade dispute and a justification for proclaiming a monopoly on the import of rice. He points out that a Government monopoly in trade means the enriching of a privileged few and that rice being the chief means of barter a Government monopoly of it would mean that the export of Maldive fish would automatically become a Government monopoly as well. The Maldive fish which the people barter for rice, like other commodities depends on its bartering value on the law of supply and demand. Ceylon being the only market for Maldive fish, the exchange value of rice in terms of Maldive fish cannot be controlled without also controlling the price of Maldive fish in Ceylon. Referring to the large amounts of vested interests he states that a Government monopoly virtually amounts to a confiscation of all the capital that has been vested by the trading interests.

Such are some of the principal points in the argument of the Borah community against the action taken by the Maldivian Government.

A considerable amount of sympathy has been evinced by the Ceylonese*, both in the Press and elsewhere, for the Maldivian Government. This is possibly due to the following reasons:—

With the advent of the new State Council in Ceylon under the Donoughmore Scheme in 1931, and the grant of male and female suffrage, the Ceylonese have begun to feel more nationally

The word Ceylonese is the general term applied to all the inhabitants of Ceylon whether Sinhalese or Tamil. The former are of Aryan and the latter of Dravidian origin. The Sinhalese are the people of Ceylon who are of Aryan origin or descent.

articulate and democratic. Naturally they are inclined to view with favour the birth of a new Constitution in a neighbouring country so closely connected with their own, and affirmed to be on a nationalistic and democratic basis which allows the people more opportunity for self-expression. The innate distaste of the Ceylonese to exploitation by the vested interests of foreigners, no matter of what nationality, makes them feel that here is a small country which has been exploited by a group of foreigners, for in Ceylon the Indian, whoever he may be, is regarded as a foreigner. The Sinhalese in particular look on the Maldivians as of the same race as theirs, descended from colonists from Ceylon. There is thus the bond of a kindred people.

In all parts of the world and in every path of life, the rich and successful man of business is looked on with envy, very often not unmixed with actual dislike.

Now, the Sinhalese as a race, which has produced some very brilliant examples in the realm of the Law, Medicine, Scientific Research, and other learned professions, has so far with few exceptions not evinced any great aptitude for business or trade. The consequence is that the non-Ceylonese merchants and business men are

Although in many instances there has been considerable admixture of blood through intermarriage the Sinhalese and Tamils are quite distinct from one another.

not always regarded with too much favour by a certain section of the Sinhalese. Their ultimate goal is for Ceylon to acquire Dominion status, if not complete independence, and to manage their own affairs without outside interference. Possibly this is a very laudable ambition for them to try and achieve, their contention being that only with full responsible government by the people of the country itself with their right to self-determination will they be able to realize their legitimate political aspirations.

How it is proposed in the event of their obtaining complete independence to preserve it "against the envy of less happier lands" is a problem to which sufficient thought has not perhaps been given. For Ceylon to maintain an army, navy and air force adequate and necessary for her own protection would be entirely beyond her resources.

Their sympathies were therefore bound to be on the side of the Maldivian Constitution as opposed to the Indian merchants though, possibly, they would be the first to resent any government by a privileged and aristocratic oligarchy as is said rightly or wrongly to be the case in the Maldives at present under their new Constitution.

To gain still further the sympathy of the Sinhalese, following the trade dispute in July, the Sultan issued the following message to be conveyed to the people of Ceylon, which is dated the 28th September, 1933.

"To the people of Ceylon, and, particularly the Sinhalese with whom the Maldivians claim kinship, though distant, I desire to offer, on behalf of the people of my Kingdom and myself, an expression of affectionate greetings and goodwill.

"It is my earnest prayer that the hope of the people of Ceylon to obtain self-government within the great British Empire will be crowned with success.

(Sgd.) Muhammad Shams-ud-Din Iskandar,
SULTAN OF THE MALDIVES."

The message was obviously, I should imagine, as are many Royal communications all the world over, an inspired one and well calculated to enlist the sympathy of the Sinhalese on the side of the Maldivian Government.

It will be seen from what has been set forth at the beginning of this chapter that the new Maldivian Constitution, with its Cabinet of Ministers and other details, was more or less an attempt to emulate the Constitution granted to Ceylon by the Donoughmore Commission which was launched in July, 1931. There is this fundamental difference, however, that whereas the latter, in spite of many objectionable features, is undoubtedly a step farther towards democratic government, the former is but a simulacrum of it

It is a curious fact that very often when a new Constitution is ushered in those in authority seek to make themselves comfortable by fixing large salaries and emoluments for themselves and by creating new posts and appointments under government and increasing salaries of government officials and employees, no matter how slender the resources or how depleted the governmental coffers may be. To meet such extra expenditure increased taxation of the people is often resorted to, which does not make for popularity.

Kamil Didi, however, mentions these increments with pride in his statement.

As regards the establishment of a steamer service I understood from Abdul Hamid Didi, the Maldivian Representative in Ceylon, whom I have known now for several years and with whom I have had several long conversations on the subject, that the intention was for the Maldivian Government to purchase a steamer and run it themselves for the benefit of the Maldivian Government and people.

As one who has been closely connected with shipping most of my life I pointed out to Abdul Hamid Didi how hard put to it are all non-subsidized steamship lines in these days, even with the vast knowledge and experience of the business they possess, to keep their vessels running, many at a heavy loss, and perhaps a very few just covering running expenses. I asked him how it was expected to run a steamer service such as was proposed by people who had no previous experience in such matters at anything but a considerable loss. I found him, however, invariably most optimistic with regard to the matter.

He used to tell me that he was convinced that a steamer service such as contemplated would prove to be not only a boon but a veritable gold mine.

Possibly he had not taken sufficiently into account that although a profit might be made with one full cargo it could hardly be expected to obtain such cargoes continuously.

There would be laying-up expenses to meet when cargo was not offering freely and other heavy items of expenditure such as docking, maintenance and repairs.

As, however, it was a scheme which he had set his heart upon I was naturally reluctant to discourage him.

Early in November, 1933, rumours of political trouble and disturbances in the Maldives reached Ceylon. Later it was reported that the trouble had not yet completely died down and that further disturbances had occurred in Male which resulted in the withdrawal to Ceylon of three Ministers.

The first Minister to arrive in Colombo was

Kamil Didi, Minister of Home Affairs. He was followed later by Husain Didi, Salahaudin, Minister of Justice, and Ibrahim Ali Didi, Minister of Health.

A conference was held at the residence of the Governor of Ceylon which was attended by Abdul Hamid Didi, the Maldivian Representative, and Amin Didi, Minister of Commerce, and the situation was discussed with the Acting Governor, Sir Graeme Tyrrell, C.M.G.

The present situation was in no way connected with the trouble that previously arose between the Borah merchants and the Government. Apparently difficulties had arisen through the eagerness of some of the Ministers to institute a number of reforms which were neither understood by nor acceptable to the people.

Abdul Hamid Didi reported that the situation was under control and many of the new enactments had been suspended.

On the 18th December, 1933, Prince Hasan Izzudin, the only son of the Sultan, who had been spending a little over two years in Ceylon which was stated to be for reasons of health, but there is little doubt that political vicissitudes were a factor as well, left Colombo for Male in the B.I.S.N. Co's. s.s. "Barjora" which had been specially chartered for the purpose by the Maldivian Government.

Shortly prior to the Prince's departure there

arrived in Ceylon two other princes, sons of the former Sultan. They had returned from Egypt where they had been living practically in exile as under the new Constitution they were entitled to come back to Male.

Accompanying Prince Izzudin on his voyage were the Maldivian Representative and the three Ministers and their staffs who had previously withdrawn to Ceylon. Also Amin Didi Effendi, the Minister of Commerce, who had gone to Colombo as an agent of his Government to interview the Ceylon Government and was not in any way involved in the political situation.

Being staunch supporters of the Prince it was apparently their intention on returning to take immediate steps to have him recognized by the people as the lawful heir-apparent and successor to the Sultan.

It is said that the Prince himself, being of a democratic nature, earnestly desired to save the new Maldivian Constitution from dissolution which was threatened on account of the over-enthusiasm of some of the young Ministers in introducing far-reaching and irritating reforms into the country before the people were prepared to receive or understand them. In short they had attempted to put new wine into old bottles, always a dangerous experiment when dealing with unsophisticated and oriental people such as the Maldivians, who are possessed of peculiarly insular and conservative ideas.

After deciding on a very conciliatory course of action they had drawn up a scheme to be presented to the Sultan on their arrival containing several modifications to the Constitution and abrogating certain regulations and ordinances to which the people had raised objection.

The Prince also intended to endeavour to prevail on the Sultan to grant a free pardon to the Ministers, their staffs, and others who had been responsible for the present impasse, and thus pave the way for the easier working of the Constitution.

In the early afternoon of December 20th, 1933, the s.s. "Barjora" arrived and anchored in the roadstead of Male; the intention apparently being that Prince Izzudin after landing was to be declared as the rightful and legal successor to his father the Sultan. This, however, had to be postponed as an order was issued prohibiting the ex-Ministers and party on board, with the exception of the Prince, from landing. The Prince, however, having presumably thrown in his lot with those on board, refused to land by himself. This was on the Wednesday, the day of the ship's arrival.

Apparently a hostile mob of several thousand had assembled on the maidan in front of the Sultan's palace which meant to offer considerable opposition, if not force, to any of the ex-Ministers in the event of their attempting to land.

After several messages and letters had been exchanged between the Sultan and his son from shore to ship the latter was at length persuaded to land alone, which he did at dawn on Friday, the 22nd December, exactly a year since the birth of the Constitution.

The ex-Ministers on board with the exception of the Minister of Commerce, Amin Didi, who landed at the express invitation of the Sultan, did not leave the ship, having elected and been allowed to return to Colombo.

The "Barjora" arrived back in Colombo on Sunday night, the 24th December. On board her was no less a person than Husain Hilmy Didi Effendi, who had been appointed by the Sultan and his Government to be the new Maldivian Government Representative in Ceylon in place of Abdul Hamid Didi.

On his return to Ceylon, in an interview with the Press, Abdul Hamid Didi is reported to have stated that "the political disaffections at Male were causing considerable anxiety and that there was in fact no law or order in the country and that even His Highness the Sultan seemed to be living in a state of continual fear of being dethroned. He was perfectly sure, however, that Prince Izzudin would bring about a settlement very soon. The Minister who complied with the

Sultan's request to land was compelled by the people to resign his Ministerial office. The others, fearing a similar fate would await them, decided to return to Colombo until the future appeared safer".

He went on to say that the Prince whose chief desire was to safeguard the new Maldivian Constitution and who was not unpopular with the people was, it was stated, well received by his subjects and had determined to stay at Male and prevail upon his father to grant a free pardon to those Ministers, their staffs, and others who were concerned in the present crisis. That to his knowledge the Ministers were not guilty of anything and he was at a loss to understand why the people were so hostile towards them. He considered that the cause of the present trouble was the result of some grave misunderstandings among the people and was all an imaginary affair.

The people, moreover, had decided to send the Ministers to the different islands with an allowance, but they refused to land as there was no guarantee of their receiving justice at the hands of the people.

Abdul Hamid Didi is quite naturally biassed in favour of the errant Ministers, but as he was living in Ceylon and not in Male at the time of the unrest his statement would appear to show that he was possibly not in possession at the time of all the facts with regard to the situation which had arisen.

On the 9th of January, 1934, a statement was issued to the Ceylon Press by Husain Hilmy Didi Effendi, the new Maldivian Representative, who was actually in Male at the time of these happenings and who is therefore I consider in a much better position to explain the reasons which led to them. His statement more or less contradicts that of his predecessor, and for the sake of clarity I quote it as written:—

"THE MALDIVIAN TROUBLES

"Will you kindly permit me the use of your hospitable columns to correct certain reports made in a recent issue of your paper concerning 'political unrest' in the Maldive Islands.

"I write to assert that there is no truth in the statement that there is no law and order in the Maldive Islands. Further, His Highness the Sultan continues to be quite popular with his people, and there are absolutely no grounds for saying that he lives in fear of dethronement. The question of the succession to the throne causes no anxiety as, under the new Constitution, the election should be made from among certain members of the Royal family by a specially convened Council of State, first consideration being given to the Sultan's eldest son.

" All that has happened is that, some time ago, three of the Ministers introduced certain unpopular and unauthorized measures. For example, various public tanks were closed and other amenities withheld: but no sufficient notice of the steps was given and no adequate substitutes were provided. Certain rules for pedestrians were instituted—again without notice. Import and export duties were increased; a price was exacted for timber from the people who had formerly received it free of charge for building boats; further, it was decided to purchase a steamer for the Government. The fiscal measures cited were in direct contravention of the new Constitution, as they did not receive the necessary sanction of the people's Assembly. Owing to wide-spread discontent these measures were repealed and the Ministers concerned were removed from office, public confidence in the new Government being thus restored. This is no parallel to Amanullah's régime in Afghanistan, as the measures that caused dissatisfaction cannot be called 'progressive'.

" On the occasion of the recent visit to Male of Prince Hasan Izzuddin and the ex-Ministers, the people were in readiness to accord the prince a warm welcome; but they were disappointed at the subsequent turn of events. A programme for the reception drawn up by Mr. E. A. H. Didi and forwarded by him to the authorities in Male roused the resentment of the latter. In the next place, when the Minister of Foreign Affairs set out to the 'Barjora' bearing a letter from the Sultan to the Prince, Mr. Didi asked him to wait in the boat while he, himself, carried the letter to the Prince. This action was regarded by the people as an insult to the Sultan's representative. On a subsequent visit of the same Minister, a bucket was lowered for the Sultan's letter; but the Minister refused to place the letter in the bucket.

"It had been decided by the Sultan that the ex-Ministers should be awarded a suitable allowance and requested to retire to certain islands not far from Male. But Prince Hasan Izzuddin refused to land except on the following conditions:—

1. That the Ministers should be pardoned and reinstated; or
2. That they should be pardoned and allowed to live in Male with their families.
3. Failing this, that they should be allowed to return to Colombo.

The last condition was accepted. The Prince landed in Male on Friday, the 22nd December.

"The Minister of Commerce was not one of the unpopular Ministers; on the other hand he is one of the most popular. He had been to Colombo on a political mission and returned to Male by the 'Barjora'. His resignation on arrival at Male was due to a misconception and was not accepted by the Sultan. He went ashore at the invitation of the Sultan and remained there of his own accord.

"The attitude of the people who assembled at the maidan was far from hostile and there were no signs of disorder or unrest as is borne out by the following extract from a letter written to me by the Commander of the 'Barjora':—

> 'In my report on my voyage I have emphasized the fact that during my stay in Male I saw nothing alarming occur and the attitude of the Ministers who interviewed me on board my ship was most courteous and friendly. In fact I could not understand the state of panic of my passengers, although that was real enough to them, and I should judge that they were most unpopular with the inhabitants of Male'."

The Lacadive Islands, which are situated north of the Maldives, are under the Government of Madras. The inhabitants are of the same race, language, and religion as the Maldivians.

Whilst not advocating for a moment that the Maldivians should be shorne of their independence or their right to self-determination it might perhaps be a wise course if the Government of Ceylon were to arrange to have a Representative in Male who could act as an intermediary between foreign traders and the Maldivian Government. He could also be an adviser when necessary to a

Constitution which is at present only experiencing its birth throes and is more or less composed of young and inexperienced legislators, impatient of delay in introducing reforms—thirty-five new enactments were promulgated in the space of less than a year—to a people who are still quite unprepared by their lack of education and their innate conservatism of either understanding or accepting them.

If this suggestion is not feasible it might be possible for periodical visits to be made by a Representative of the Ceylon Government to Male.

After all, if the Maldivians find it necessary to have their Representative in Ceylon to protect their interests, there is no reason why the Ceylon Government should not do likewise with regard to the Maldives. Let us hope, however, that matters will now settle down peacefully and that happiness and contentment will return once more to these hardy sons of the sea in the Maldivian Archipelago.

CHAPTER X

UNDER THE WHITE ENSIGN

TUESDAY is a day that has had a curious influence on my life. With me it has not necessarily implied a lucky day, but many events which have been of peculiar significance to me have occurred so often on a Tuesday that I have really begun to look on it as a day of fate.

To give only a few instances—it was on a Tuesday that I first saw the light. It was on a Tuesday that I left Scotland to go out to India. It was on the same day of the week that my mother died, and some few years later my father also died on a Tuesday.

I left India after a residence of over twenty years in that country on my transfer to Ceylon on a Tuesday and arrived in Colombo to assume my new duties on the following Tuesday. In 1927 I had the honour of being a guest on board H.M.S. "Effingham", the Flag Ship of the East Indies Squadron, when she sailed from Colombo homeward bound, also on a Tuesday.

I could give numerous other instances of the significance of this day of the week to me.

By the courtesy and kindness of Capt. R. B. Darke, D.S.O., R.N., of H.M.S. "Enterprise", I was invited to proceed in his ship on one of the periodical visits paid by British war ships to the Maldives. I gladly accepted his kind offer as it would give me an opportunity of seeing Male once more after a period of eight years, during which time many things had happened. The original date of departure from Colombo was fixed for Monday, the 2nd April, 1934. Later, H.E. The Governor of Ceylon, Sir Edward Stubbs, G.C.M.G., expressed his desire to visit the Maldives in the "Enterprise". The ship's sailing date was subsequently changed to Tuesday the 3rd April.

And now I have begun to write the last chapter of this book on Tuesday, the 10th April, 1934.

I was on board soon after seven o'clock on the morning of the 3rd April in order not to be in the way when His Excellency came on board which he did shortly after eight o'clock, accompanied by his Private Secretary and A.D.C., and also my friend Husain Hilmy Didi Effendi, the Maldivian Representative in Ceylon.

The Captain greeted me most kindly and told off someone to show me the quarters assigned to me.

Sharp at 8.30 a.m. the ship quietly slipped from her moorings, abreast of the Flag Ship H.M.S. "Hawkins" and we were steaming out of

Colombo Harbour. The weather was perfect and the sea calm, with a moderate wind from the south-west. As we passed several merchant ships lying in the harbour, some discharging and others taking in cargo, they dipped their flags.

The rest of the day was uneventful.

I woke at five next morning when the bugle sounded the reveille. I went on deck. There was hardly a sound except the swish of water against the ship's sides. Dawn had not broken, the moon was waning but Jupiter on our starboard bow and Venus, the morning star, on our port quarter, shone with marvellous brilliance.

By ten o'clock we sighted the first islands of the group near Male on our starboard beam. One or two of these are inhabited, but not the others. At eleven o'clock we had slowed down and were now abreast of the southern shore of Male.

We passed through the gateway of Male, the island of Hulule, on our starboard beam and Male on our port side, and entered Male harbour by 11.30 a.m.

Hilmy had told me he had not expected we would reach Male before the morning of the 5th April, and had previously advised his Government accordingly. As we were a day beforehand he wondered whether all preparations for His Excellency's visit would have been completed in time. However, his fears in this respect were quickly dispelled.

The town itself was gaily decorated with flags and the five buggalows and three schooners lying at anchor in the harbour were all dressed.

A salute of twenty-one guns boomed out from the ship and immediately afterwards this was replied to by a similar number from the shore battery.

At noon a State boat came alongside with the Maldivian Ministers who had come to call on and pay their respects to the Governor. Everyone in the ship was enchanted with the magnificent colour effects. A turquoise blue sky flecked with white clouds above. The islands like uncut emeralds, the long line of silvery-white foam breaking on the coral reefs in the distance. Streaks of the most lovely shade of jade round the islands merging into the dark sapphire blue of the sea. I had seen it all before myself, but this did not prevent me from appreciating it to the full once more.

At 1.30 p.m. I had the honour of having lunch with His Excellency and found him to be a man of most charming personality. Hilmy had also been invited to join the party but was unable to do so having had to go ashore in connection with the preparations for His Excellency's reception.

At three o'clock the State Barge with the Sultan on board arrived. The barge was manned by twelve oarsmen dressed in white and wearing scarlet tarbushes. The orders were all carried out with precision by whistle which the boat's coxswain carried on him.

At the bow was a purple flag of silk and astern the Maldivian flag, scarlet edged, with emerald green centre, and white star. A guard of marines was stationed on the quarter-deck.

An exchange of compliments took place between His Highness the Sultan and His Excellency the Governor. The guard was duly inspected and then the Sultan took his departure. The ship fired a salute of seventeen guns.

It was the first time I had seen the Sultan, and I had an excellent view of him as he came up the gangway of the ship. He is a man of middle height and about fifty-five years of age. He looks strongly built and carries his age well. He was dressed in a flowing *jelab* of light brown silk and wore a white turban in the Arab fashion.

At four o'clock the State Barge returned to the ship to convey His Excellency ashore to return the Sultan's visit. On this occasion the Governor's flag was flown at the bow. After the interview with the Sultan at the palace the Governor returned on board in the ship's motor boat, the shore batteries firing a salute of seventeen guns.

His Excellency presented a very fine wireless receiving set to the Sultan which I understand is to be installed in the palace. This, besides being

(*Upper*) H.M.S. "ENTERPRISE," COLOMBO HARBOUR.

(*Lower*) THE SULTAN'S STATE BARGE

a means of recreation, should prove useful in keeping Male in touch with the outside world.

Shortly before six o'clock I received a visit from Muhammad Farid Didi Effendi, the Prime Minister, Hasan Farid Didi, his brother, Minister of Finance and Foreign Affairs, Amin Didi Effendi, Minister of Commerce, and Ibrahim Didi Effendi, Minister of Health and Agriculture.

Hasan Farid Didi I had last met in London in 1927, where he had gone to complete his education, and it was pleasant to recall our last meeting.

They were all very anxious for me to go ashore with them that evening, but as it was getting dark and I had had rather a long day I thanked them and suggested I should come ashore next morning about eight, to which they agreed and promised to send a special boat for me.

That night, about eight, the ship's searchlights played on the harbour and the town. The effect of the light on the surf in the distance was most weirdly fascinating.

Punctually at eight o'clock next morning a boat arrived alongside for me and I landed in Male shortly before half-past eight. I was met at the jetty by Hilmy himself and the four Ministers, who accorded me a warm welcome.

I noticed many changes and improvements since my last visit. A fine new Custom House has been erected in the vicinity of the landing jetty, and a large Government rice store near by.

Lines of new shops all very neat and clean have been built where a brisk trade seems to be carried on. The shop-keepers, too, are Maldivians and were most polite.

Some of the shops had gramophones which could be heard playing some of the latest Hindustani vocal and instrumental records.

The Sultan himself, too, is I believe very fond of gramophone music and possesses thousands of records which he has had purchased for him from time to time.

All these improvements were instituted and carried out by Amir Abdul Majid Didi Ranna Banderi Kilegefan before he left Male and he certainly deserves the greatest credit for the work he has done on behalf of his royal master and his people.

We then went to the house of the Prime Minister which he has recently had built. It is a flat-roofed two-storied building rather in the Egyptian style which one sees in Cairo. A small but beautifully arranged garden with a fish-pond and surrounded by a wall stands at one side of the house.

After cigarettes and coffee I decided to have a stroll and also to take some photographs. Hilmy and the Ministers having to receive the Governor when he paid an unofficial visit at ten o'clock, Ibrahim Hilmy Didi Effendi, Hilmy's younger brother, was very kindly deputed by Hilmy to act as my guide. I found young Ibrahim a charming boy and very well informed. He is a student at Aligarh College in India where he is studying medicine with a view eventually of returning to Male and practising there. He was on vacation at the time but was expecting to return to India in May.

Among other places we visited Hilmy's office where I had first met him. Many additions and improvements had been made but the old study was just as it was with the writing table and the well-stocked book-cases.

After drinking some cool sherbet which was very welcome as the day promised to be hot we walked along to the Idu Miskit which I was anxious to see again, and to examine the stone carving at its base.

Every road in Male was decorated with red flags—the Maldivian colour—and with numerous triumphal arches. The whole road up from the jetty and leading to the palace—about three hundred yards—had a gay canopy spread over it, and flags and other decorations on either side.

A seaplane from the ship soared up into the sky, looking in the brilliant sunlight like a gigantic silver bird. Now and again the roar of its engines could be heard as it swept down to a lower altitude. Although it was not the first time that the inhabitants of Male had seen a similar machine it nevertheless seemed to fascinate them, and on every road men, women and children could be seen emerging from their houses to stand and gaze at this wonder in the sky.

Again I was impressed with the wonderful condition in which the roads are kept and the clean white coral sand. The flags and decorations were of course in honour of the Governor, but the roads are always kept in the same perfect condition. In many places I noticed that the *cadjan* walls had been replaced by brick.

As on my previous visit the women and children came to the doors and stood about, but I had only to put my hand on the camera bag when they darted inside like frightened birds, and although young Ibrahim and I used every persuasion I found it impossible to obtain a snapshot of them. In the afternoon several of the ship's officers who landed in Male met with the same experience, much to their chagrin.

We visited El Habshi's shrine at the eastern end of the island and here there is an uninterrupted view of the huge surf breakers crashing on the coral barrier reef and glittering in the sunshine. Thence we strolled along the ramparts. Once more I was struck with the wonderful fertility of the soil. In many a small garden mango trees were laden with fruit. Coconut palms flourished and the leaves of plantain trees waved lazily in the breeze. Crotons of various colours grew profusely and many other beautiful shrubs and flowering trees.

Presumably with a view to creating a more tidy appearance, I noticed that most of the old guns had been removed from the embrasures along the walls of Male, leaving these quite bare, and had been stacked outside the walls. Some few were still mounted. A few of the guns bore the crown of Portugal, now nearly obliterated by time and weather.

I took the opportunity of visiting my old quarters where I stayed on the occasion of my previous visit. The house has been converted into a Government dispensary and is in charge of a very efficient Tamil apothecary from Jaffna —Mr. Arumanayagam. I congratulated him on the clean and orderly condition of his dispensary for which he deserves great credit. He told me that the dispensary was very much appreciated by the people. Most of the cases he had to deal with were malarial fever.

I was glad to see that the seed I had sown when I first visited Male with regard to the establishment of a dispensary on up-to-date lines had borne fruit. Incidentally, too, I discovered that the apothecary was a close relative of an accountant clerk in my office in Colombo.

Later, in conversation with the Ministers, I suggested that other young men should emulate Ibrahim Hilmy Didi's example and proceed to Ceylon, India, or Europe and study medicine and surgery, as they would undoubtedly be of real use to the people on their return. I had made the same suggestion on my previous visit.

Prince Izzudin, the Sultan's son, was unfortunately down with fever and was unable to be present at any of the functions.

The people all seemed very contented and happy, and I noticed many carrying umbrellas and wearing shoes in the streets. On enquiry, I was told that the old law prohibiting these had been rescinded. The Sultan, far from going in fear of being dethroned as was reported some little time back, is on the contrary very much respected and loved by the people.

As everything is now perfectly quiet and no further disturbances are anticipated, now that the cause of them has been removed, the police force has been disbanded as unnecessary in view of the law-abiding character of the people and also as a measure of economy. The number of Ministers, too, has now been reduced to four and the present Cabinet consists of Muhammad Farid Didi Effendi, Prime Minister and Minister of Home Affairs and Defence; Hasan Farid Didi Effendi, Minister of Finance, Foreign Affairs and of Public Works. Both of these are sons of Amir Abdul Majid Didi, the former Prime Minister and Treasurer of the Maldives—the "Maldivian Mussolini". Muhammad Amin Didi Effendi, Minister of Commerce and

Education, is the son of my old friend Ahmad Didi Effendi, the brother of Abdul Majid.

Alas ! I was unable to meet Ahmad Didi as I learned from his son that he was at present in Madras undergoing medical treatment, and that he was very far from well. Amin, his son, in addition to his other duties, has taken his father's place meanwhile and is Acting Private Secretary to His Highness the Sultan.

The fourth Minister is Ibrahim Didi Effendi, the Minister of Health and Agriculture. The acting Minister of Justice and Endowments is Bodu Fenwaluge Seedi.

I learned, too, that one of the three deported Ministers, Ibrahim Ali Didi Effendi, had recently returned to Male from Colombo and had been sent to Toddu Island in the vicinity of Male on an allowance. The two other Ministers, viz., Husain Didi Salahaudin, formerly Minister of Justice, and Ahmad Kamil Didi, the ex-Minister for Home Affairs and Education, were still living in Colombo, not having ventured to return.

I was also given to understand that it was the Deputy to the Finance Minister who was in a great measure responsible for the trouble between the Maldivian Government and the Borah merchants.

I heard to my surprise but on the best of authority that the letter purporting to have emanated from His Highness the Sultan and addressed to the people of Ceylon dated the 28th September, 1933, which appeared in the Ceylon Press and which I quoted in the previous chapter, had not been sent from Male at all. The Sultan, indeed, was quite ignorant of it and in any case would never have sent it, as His Highness is most averse to associate himself in any way with the politics of any country outside his own.

The former Maldivian Representative, Abdul Hamid Didi Effendi, who was replaced by Husain Hilmy Didi Effendi, has been granted a pension by the Sultan and is residing in Ceylon.

I had the opportunity of meeting one of the few remaining lacquer workers in Male and also of seeing him engraving some of his work with artistic skill.

I later pointed out to the Minister of Commerce that this beautiful craftsmanship should not be allowed to die out but should rather be encouraged by the State and in the schools if possible, as I felt sure it would by its very perfection and beauty always command a ready sale in Colombo and elsewhere.

I returned to the ship at 1.30 p.m. as the heat and glare at midday was intense. Before doing so, however, I called on some of my old Borah friends who were delighted to see me again. They all seemed very happy and contented and told me that everything was going on very smoothly. They mentioned, however, that there had been more or less a glut of fish during the past season and that this, coupled with the depression and consequent lack of demand, had been the cause of a very considerable drop in the prices obtainable in Ceylon for Maldive fish. In many instances their Colombo houses had sustained heavy losses on their sales.

Nearby their shops I saw the new mosque they had erected, which was quite an imposing building.

In the afternoon we watched a boat race from the ship. Fifteen craft took part. These were sailing boats or *dhonis,* about twenty feet in length, lateen rigged. In the brilliant sunshine and the blue sea around, with green islands as a background, they looked like white sea birds. The *dhoni* belonging to Amin Didi, Minister of Commerce, won easily after a very exciting race. She was able to sail very close to the wind and led the whole way, from start to finish.

A silver cup was presented by His Excellency the Governor to the winner, who seemed very pleased and proud of it.

The next morning, Friday, was cloudy, and rain threatened. I went ashore at nine o'clock as I was anxious to see the Sultan's procession in state to the Hukuru Miskit for prayers.

Meanwhile I was invited by Amin Didi Effendi to his father's house where he also resides, and we had coffee and cigarettes. I remembered the old house well, for it was there that I many a time had tea and long conversations with his charming old father, Ahmad Didi. A slight shower of rain fell but soon passed, and I was now filling in the time till midday when the procession was to leave the palace.

I walked down to the Custom House and shortly after arriving there I saw the ship's motor boat come to the jetty. Out of it stepped the Governor's Private Secretary and his A.D.C. Thinking that they, too, had come to see the procession I approached them and was surprised to learn that they bore a letter from His Excellency to the Sultan informing the latter that owing to the serious illness of one of the ship's petty officers the "Enterprise" would be leaving within an hour and that His Excellency regretted in the circumstances he would be unable to receive the Sultan on board at 2.30 p.m., as previously arranged, to say farewell.

Having said good-bye to the Ministers and my other friends it was not long before I was speeding back to the ship. Hilmy had had to change from his Maldivian dress to European clothes in record time I should imagine, for he came along with us.

Before the ship sailed the Sultan sent quite a boat-load of presents alongside for His Excellency the Governor, and the Captain and Officers of the ship. These consisted chiefly of fine Maldivian lacquer ware and rolls of beautiful Maldivian mats and also a variety of fruit.

East of Male lies the uninhabited island of Funadu, not far from Hulule, which is inhabited. Near Funadu is another small island, Dunidu, where the wrecks of buggalows can still be seen.

It is a curious fact how the bones of the British are scattered all over the world, very often in most unlooked for and lonely places.

On this little island of Funadu is a double grave on the opposite side of the landing place. It is approached by a clear-cut path, well sanded, which traverses a small plantation. The graves are enclosed by a low brick wall about two and a half feet in height. The width of the enclosure is five feet and the length thirteen feet. There are two headstones, each about three feet high. One of these bears no inscription, but is presumed to be that of a British soldier. The other stone bears the following inscription:—

Sacred to the Memory of
PRIVATE VICTOR LUCKSHAM,
R.M.L.I.
H.M.S. "Prosperpine".
Drowned while bathing at Hulule, near Male,
9th August, 1909.
Aged 24 years.

It is to the credit of the Sultan and his Government that these graves are so well tended and looked after.

The ship sailed at one o'clock, and in order to reach Colombo by midday on Saturday her speed was increased to eighteen knots.

Soon the green islands and atolls disappeared one by one and melted into the horizon. We experienced a heavy rain-shower in the afternoon and the sky was overcast with clouds.

We had drenching rain the first part of the evening, but later on the weather cleared and the stars shone out.

A voyage in a King's ship is an unforgettable experience. I shall always look back with gratitude to the kindness I received from the Captain and his Officers and, in fact, from all on board with whom I came in contact.

Sailor-men, as I mentioned in a previous chapter, all over the world are the very soul of kindness and consideration, and in this the British sailor stands *nulli secundus.*

There are many interesting customs and ceremonials in a war-ship, but the one which always thrills me most is the hoisting of the White Ensign at eight o'clock in the morning. The band of the Marines stands ready with their instruments on the quarter deck. Punctual to the minute the Flag is slowly hoisted to the strains of " God Save the King ", and as the last note is played the White Ensign has reached the top of the flagstaff, and floats out on the breeze. One cannot help feeling that inward pride of race which is the heritage of the British.

I had the pleasure of meeting two interesting personalities on board, viz., H.R.H. Prince Juan, Crown Prince and heir-apparent of H.M. King Alfonso of Spain, and Prince Vudhujai of the Royal House of Siam, who were serving as midshipman and naval cadet respectively in the ship. Prince Juan I had known for some time previously. To both could the name "Prince Charming" be equally applicable, and when I have said this nothing more needs to be added.

The speed of the ship was eased down on Saturday morning, and by noon Colombo Harbour was sighted. As we steamed into harbour the Governor's launch met us and came alongside.

At half-past one the Governor took his leave of the ship and descended the gangway into the launch. His flag was hoisted and then the ship's guns gave him a salute of seventeen guns.

Thus ended what was to me a most memorable and enjoyable voyage.

The following day, Sunday, there arrived in the P. & O. R.M.S. "Corfu" from Bombay no less a person than Amir Abdul Majid Didi.

I did not meet him that day but Hilmy arranged an interview for me with him on the following evening. We were both mutually glad to meet each other and talked of many things in Hindustani as he does not speak English. He told me he was returning to Male at the request of the Sultan. I expressed my pleasure at hearing this and told him that his country was in real need of a strong and experienced man like him, and I wished him every success.

The four Ministers I met were all very charming young men, but one could not help feeling that their youth and inexperience was rather a handicap and that some one with more age and experience was needed to guide the destinies of this island race.

Amir Abdul Majid Didi on his return will supply the necessary ballast, I feel sure, and under his able guidance the Government will be carried on for the benefit of the people and also for those who trade with the islands, which after all is the essence of good government.

INDEX

INDEX

INDEX